# IRAN'S
# Security Policy
## in the Post-Revolutionary Era

Daniel Byman · Shahram Chubin · Anoushiravan Ehteshami · Jerrold Green

Prepared for the Office of the Secretary of Defense

Approved for public release; distribution unlimited

National Defense Research Institute
**RAND**

The research described in this report was sponsored by the Department of Defense. The research was conducted in RAND's National Defense Research Institute, a federally funded research and development center supported by the Office of the Secretary of Defense, the Joint Staff, the unified commands, and the defense agencies under Contract DASW01-01-C-0004.

**Library of Congress Cataloging-in-Publication Data**

Iran's security policy in the post-revolutionary era / Daniel L. Byman ... [et al.].
    p. cm.
    MR-1320
    Includes bibliographical references.
    ISBN 0-8330-2971-1
    1. Iran—Military policy. 2. National security—Iran. 3. Iran—Politics and government—1979– I. Byman, Daniel, 1967–

UA853.I7 I72 2001
355' 033055—dc21

                    2001020486

Cover photographs are reprinted from http://www.khamenei.com/martyrs-photogallery.htm

RAND is a nonprofit institution that helps improve policy and decisionmaking through research and analysis. RAND® is a registered trademark. RAND's publications do not necessarily reflect the opinions or policies of its research sponsors.

Published 2001 by RAND
1700 Main Street, P.O. Box 2138, Santa Monica, CA 90407-2138
1200 South Hayes Street, Arlington, VA 22202-5050
201 North Craig Street, Suite 102, Pittsburgh, PA 15213-1516
RAND URL: http://www.rand.org/
To order RAND documents or to obtain additional information, contact Distribution Services: Telephone: (310) 451-7002;
Fax: (310) 451-6915; Internet: order@rand.org

# PREFACE

This report assesses Iran's security policy. It examines broad drivers of Iran's security policy, describes important security institutions, explores decisionmaking, and reviews Iran's relations with key countries. It concludes by assessing the characteristics that distinguish Iran's security policy today.

This study's findings will be of greatest interest to analysts and scholars who seek to anticipate changes in Iran's behavior or to understand the more opaque developments in Iran. This study will also be of interest to policymakers, who will be better able to adapt U.S. policy to meet the challenges posed by Iran today and in the future.

This research was conducted for the Department of Defense within the Center for International Security and Defense Policy of RAND's National Defense Research Institute, a federally funded research and development center sponsored by the Office of the Secretary of Defense, the Joint Staff, the Unified Commands, and the defense agencies.

# CONTENTS

# TABLES

The sources of Iran's security policy defy simple explanation. Religion, nationalism, ethnicity, economics, and geopolitics all are important factors explaining Iran's goals and tactics in its relationship with the outside world. So too are the agendas of key security institutions and the ambitions of their leaders. The picture is even more confusing because Iran's politics and even its basic structure of government are in flux. The 1997 election of Mohammed Khatami as the country's president triggered a struggle among Iran's political elite that has changed the political debate in Iran. Therefore, it is often difficult to understand, much less predict, Iranian decision-making.

## FUNDAMENTAL SOURCES OF SECURITY POLICY

Iran's security policy is often described as a blend of Islamic and nationalist objectives. Both these factors, however, have carried less weight in recent years than have more standard political considerations. Geopolitics has reasserted its importance, and economics has grown from a foreign policy irrelevance to a leading factor. Ethnicity and other communal divisions also drive Iran's security policy, particularly with regard to the countries on Iran's borders. Preserving regional stability and improving Iran's economy have forced the clerical regime to cultivate neighboring governments, even at the expense of revolutionary principles. As a result of this shift, the Islamic Republic often favors far more cautious policies than its Islamic and nationalist ethos might otherwise dictate.

## SECURITY POLICY ACTORS AND DECISIONMAKING

Myriad individuals, institutions, and organizations play important political and military roles in Iran. For issues of security policy, several organizations are particularly important. These include the intelligence services, the Islamic Revolutionary Guard Corps (IRGC), and the regular armed forces, or *Artesh*. The *Artesh* has become an increasingly important player in recent years, often at the expense of the IRGC.

In general, the various institutions emphasize different issues, to their mutual satisfaction, though in practice they overlap considerably in their duties and beliefs. The intelligence services and the IRGC are far more focused on the defense of the revolution from its internal enemies than is the *Artesh*. In contrast, the *Artesh* focuses its efforts on more traditional threats, such as an Iraqi attack.

Iran's formal security structure is not reflected in actual decisionmaking. Formally, the Supreme Leader oversees Iran's security policy, while the President is responsible for much of the day-to-day decisionmaking. Informally, however, the Supreme Leader exercises considerable control over the daily implementation of policy. Many institutions often share the responsibility for formulating and implementing particular policies, leading to duplication and rivalry. In addition, most institutions in Iran are weak, while the personal networks of leaders are strong. Power thus shifts according to the fortunes of individual leaders rather than to the purviews of institutions.

Iran's decisionmaking is characterized by two competing trends—seemingly chaotic complexity and consensus. The large number of institutional and noninstitutional actors, family ties, personal relationships, overlapping institutional authority, and the mixture of religion and politics all contrive to make it difficult to identify who has a say on what issue. While there is a formal system for decisionmaking, it is often ignored or bypassed in favor of an informal, parallel system. Individuals are constantly tempted to ignore the system, particularly if it is easier to gain a consensus that way. This complexity is balanced, however, by a cultural and procedural emphasis on consensus. Informally, there are often rules—known to the participants if not to outsiders—that govern behavior among elites. What appears as chaos to outsiders is often a highly stylized and ritualized mode of interaction. A willingness to horse trade and otherwise swap support on an ad hoc basis also preserves some solidarity. To preserve the consensus, few actors dare conduct important operations without at least the tacit approval of the senior leadership.

The result is often a constant back-and-forth process. Individuals can withhold their support, preventing significant change even if it has majority support. Different institutions that are not equally enthusiastic about change may implement policies inconsistently or unevenly, leading to mixed signals in Iran's foreign policy. In addition, policy slippage regularly occurs due to the constant renegotiation of controversial issues.

## THE MILITARY AND IRANIAN POLITICS UNDER KHATAMI

The social and political reform process unleashed by President Khatami is now a bone of contention within the defense establishment, raising the prospect of military intervention in Iranian politics. Military officers' attitudes toward popular unrest have been decidedly mixed, and their overall response has been inconsistent. While the regular forces try to make a virtue of being apolitical, there are those among the IRGC who have threatened intervention if the Islamic system is threatened by reformers. The traditional leadership's dependence on coercion is likely to increase as political tensions, infighting, and prolonged economic difficulties increase the regime's reliance on its coercive machinery. Many IRGC officers, and the vast majority of the rank and file, however, support President Khatami and his reform agenda.

There is little chance that the IRGC would rebel against its political masters and decide to find its own solution to Iran's security or political problems. The traditional elements of the regime, however, are increasingly uncertain of the IRGC's loyalty, particularly its willingness to respond rapidly and decisively during a confrontation with reformers. In response, they have created several special units designed to quell domestic unrest.

## KEY OBSERVATIONS ABOUT SECURITY POLICY

Iraq is widely recognized as the leading threat to the Islamic regime: It is the only state considered a danger to Iran's territorial integrity, because of its revisionist ambitions toward Arab parts of Iran and the Shatt al-Arab. Afghanistan is also emerging as a leading threat, given the Taliban's support for Sunni Islamic radicalism and avowed hostility toward Iran.

In general, Iran's friendships are at best lukewarm. Iran has close relations with Syria and strong working ties to Pakistan and Russia. Yet these bonds are not deep, and relations with Pakistan in particular have been fraying.

Iran's policies toward its neighbors are increasingly prudent, with the Islamic Republic trying to calm regional tension and end its isolation. Particularly near Iran's own borders, the Islamic regime has supported the status quo with regard to territorial integrity, has avoided major military provocations, and has shown a preference for working with governments over substate movements—a classic post-revolutionary era shift. Tehran has made a particular point of wooing the Gulf states and encouraging stability in Central Asia, even if this requires slighting local Islamist movements. Although Iran still supports Shi'a radicals and other Islamists throughout the world—and champions the anti-Israel front—its motives and its priorities are increasingly dictated by cold national interest concerns.

Iran's policies toward Israel and the United States are often an exception to its overall shift toward prudence. Restrictions on relations with both countries remain one of the strongest parts of the revolutionary legacy.

In general, Iran's domestic, foreign, and security policies cannot be neatly separated. All of Iran's major policy decisions involve a complex calculus of Iran's overall vulnerability, the regime's need to stay in power, and Iran's commitment to revolutionary ideals. For much of the revolutionary leadership, defending the revolutionary order often is a priority in Tehran's relationship with its neighbors and the United States.

Iran's security forces, particularly the regular military, are often voices of restraint. Iran's security forces prefer shows of force over active confrontations.  When tensions with several neighbors have escalated, Iran's military forces have conducted maneuvers and buildups near the respective areas of conflict but have deliberately sought to avoid open confrontations.  The military forces fear that almost any broad conflict would be costly and deeply unpopular.

Differences between Iran's regular armed forces and its revolutionary armed forces are decreasing.  As their commitment to professionalism has grown, and their Islamist ardor waned, the revolutionary forces have increasingly conducted business in a manner similar to that of the regular forces.

In general, Iran's security forces respect and follow the wishes of Iran's civilian leadership, even though they vigorously champion their own agendas whenever possible.  Conducting "rogue operations," or otherwise acting without civilian approval, is rare to nonexistent.

Audiences at the Department of Defense, the State Department, CENTCOM, and other government agencies provided useful feedback. Michael Eisenstadt critiqued an earlier version of this report, correcting many errors and improving its overall quality. Tom McNaugher of RAND provided an excellent review that clarified our thinking considerably. Stuart Johnson helped manage this project and ensure its quality. Risha Henneman and Renee Almassizadeh provided invaluable administrative support.

Given the sensitive nature of this report, many of those interviewed asked not to be named. Our thanks to them all.

| | |
|---|---|
| CENTCOM | U.S. Central Command |
| CWC | Chemical Weapons Convention |
| GCC | Gulf Cooperation Council |
| GDP | gross domestic product |
| IPO | Islamic Propagation Organization |
| IRGC | Islamic Revolutionary Guard Corps |
| KDP | Kurdish Democratic Party |
| MKO | *Mujahedin-e Khalq* Organization |
| MODAFL | Ministry of Defense and Armed Forces Logistics |
| MOIS | Ministry of Intelligence and Security |
| NATO | North Atlantic Treaty Organization |
| NBC | nuclear, biological, and chemical |
| OPEC | Organization of Petroleum Exporting Countries |
| PKK | Kurdish Workers' Party |
| PUK | Patriotic Union of Kurdistan |
| R&D | research and development |
| SCIRI | Supreme Council of the Islamic Revolution in Iraq |

| SCNS | Supreme Council for National Security |
| SSM | surface-to-surface missile |
| UAE | United Arab Emirates |
| UN | United Nations |
| WMD | weapons of mass destruction |

# Chapter One

# INTRODUCTION

Iranian security policy defies simple explanation. Religion, nationalism, ethnicity, economics, and geopolitics all are important factors influencing Iran's goals and tactics in its relationship with the outside world. So too are the agendas of key security institutions and the ambitions of their leaders. If anything, Iran's foreign policy is becoming more complex. The Islamic Republic, long a source of instability in the Middle East, is itself under severe pressure to change.

Iran's politics and even basic structure of government are in flux. The 1997 election of Mohammed Khatami as president triggered a struggle between reformers and revolutionaries that has changed the political debate in Iran. Because Iranian politics today are not predictable, this study focuses on the more fundamental sources of Iran's foreign policy. Although the relative priority that different leaderships would give to them varies, these sources are likely to remain important factors that drive decisionmaking under most conceivable future governments.

This study seeks to untangle this complex skein of motivations. Through an analysis of recent Iranian foreign policy, we identify the ideological and nonideological stimuli to Iranian decisionmaking and to important institutional inputs. Such an understanding will aid the United States as its troubled relationship with the Islamic Republic continues to evolve.

## KEY OBSERVATIONS

Although most of this study focuses on describing decisionmaking and the particular outcomes that characterize Iran's security policy, several broader observations (discussed in the final chapter of this report) deserve notice:

- Domestic, foreign, and security policies cannot be separated. All of Iran's major policy decisions involve a complex calculus of Iran's overall vulnerability, its need to ensure the regime stays in power, and its commitment to revolutionary ideals. Iran's leaders weigh all these factors when making their decisions.

- The Islamic Republic is increasingly prudent. Particularly near Iran's own borders, the Islamic regime has tended to support the status quo with regard to territorial integrity, has avoided major military provocations, and has shown a preference for working with governments over substate movements.

- Iran's policies toward Israel and the United States are often an exception to its overall shift toward prudence. Restrictions on relations with both countries remain one of the strongest remnants of the revolutionary legacy.

- Differences between Iran's regular armed forces and its revolutionary armed forces are decreasing. As their commitment to professionalism has grown, and their Islamist ardor waned, the revolutionary forces have increasingly conducted business in a manner similar to that of the regular forces.

- Iran's ideology is often a mask for realpolitik. Iran still supports Shi'a radicals and other Islamists throughout the world—and champions the anti-Israel front—but its motives and its priorities are increasingly dictated by cold national interest concerns.

- In general, Iran's security forces respect and follow the wishes of Iran's civilian leadership, even though they vigorously champion their own agendas whenever possible. Conducting "rogue operations," or otherwise acting without civilian approval, is rare to nonexistent.

- Iran's decisionmaking, while often chaotic, is not anarchic. There are rules to Iran's decisionmaking on major security issues, but the rules appear to be in constant flux and are informal, if well known.  On most issues, many important players have a voice.  In addition, the system emphasizes consensus, preventing individuals or small numbers of institutions from dominating overall policy.

- Iran's security institutions have overlapping responsibilities, which leads to inconsistent implementation of the same directives.  However, the emphasis on consensus, along with the relative lack of military autonomy, prevents too much deviation from agreed-upon objectives.

- The leaderships of Iran's security forces, particularly of the regular military, are often voices of restraint.  Iran's security forces prefer shows of force to active confrontations.  When tensions with several neighbors have escalated, Iran's military forces have conducted maneuvers and buildups near the respective areas of conflict but have deliberately sought to avoid open confrontations.  The military forces fear that almost any broad conflict would be costly and deeply unpopular.

To support these arguments and to gain a broader understanding of Iran's security policy, this report takes several tacks.  First, it discusses the basic drivers of Iran's security policy, including a range of ideological, strategic, and domestic factors, all of which play into Iran's decisionmaking.  Second, it looks at the particular agendas of various security institutions, particularly the regular armed forces (the *Artesh*) and the Islamic Revolutionary Guard Corps (IRGC).  Third, it explores how these drivers and agendas interact, examining Iranian decisionmaking on security issues.  Fourth, it assesses the actual outputs of Iran's security policy—relations with key states and policies on important issues, such as Iran's support for coreligionists abroad—and explores the interplay of factors that shape Iran's behavior.

Taken together, these four approaches shed light on Iran's overall security policy methods, objectives, and characteristics.

## METHODOLOGY . . . AND CAVEATS

The data for this study draw on a range of sources.  Most important, we relied on interviews with knowledgeable Iranians in the United

States, in Europe, and in Iran itself. Almost all these individuals asked not to be identified by name. We also drew on media coverage of events in Iran, again relying on both Iranian and Western sources. Finally, we used existing scholarly works to supplement the findings.

Although this report relies primarily on interviews, these have several inherent limits. First, many of those interviewed had information that was at best indirectly received. It was often impossible for us to verify the information beyond checking it with other individuals interviewed and with our own knowledge of events. Second, the subject of this report is highly sensitive. Iran, like many countries, does not have an open debate on many key civil-military issues. As a result, information was often scarce. Third, many of those interviewed almost certainly pushed their own agendas and biases. We tried to filter these out, but perfection on this score is impossible.

Several other caveats are in order. Understanding Iran's security decisionmaking is difficult at best for outside analysts. Iran's behavior often appears inconsistent, and its decisionmaking style—due to its complexity—confuses outsiders. One consistent finding of this report was the importance of individual personalities and personal networks in setting policy. Unearthing the particulars of each key individual, however, was beyond the scope of this report. Even more important, Iran's entire political system is in flux. Many of the rules that have applied for the first two decades of the Islamic Republic no longer apply or are honored more in the breach. Thus, the conclusions of this report should be reconsidered as time goes on and more data come in.

## STRUCTURE

The remainder of this study has six chapters. Chapter Two identifies deep sources of Iranian foreign policy, noting how factors such as geopolitics, religion, nationalism, ethnicity, and economics affect Iran's foreign policy goals and behavior. Chapter Three focuses on the characteristics of security decisionmaking in Iran. Chapter Four describes key security institutions and their agendas. In Chapter Five, the changing and ambiguous relationship between Iran's security institutions and Iranian society is explored. Chapter Six describes the impact of the above sources of foreign policy on Iran's behavior. This study concludes with Chapter Seven, which draws general observations on Iran's security policy.

# Chapter Two

# FUNDAMENTAL SOURCES OF IRANIAN FOREIGN AND SECURITY POLICIES

Certain characteristics of the Islamic Republic drive its foreign policy, affecting both its overall objectives and the manner in which it pursues them. Twenty years after the Islamic revolution, Islam remains the characteristic that receives the most attention, with Persian nationalism often cited as a competing source of Iran's inspiration. While Islam and nationalism are important drivers, their importance has diminished, and evolved, as Iran's revolutionary enthusiasm has given over to the pragmatic concerns that all states must take into account. Geopolitics has reasserted its importance, and economics has grown from a foreign policy irrelevance to a leading factor. Ethnicity and other communal considerations also drive Iran's foreign policy, leading the Islamic Republic to adopt far more conservative policies than its Islamic and nationalist ethos might otherwise dictate.

This chapter explores these factors and notes their relative importance. It argues that, today, the fundamental drivers of Iran's foreign policy favor caution and prudence over the adventurism that characterized the Islamic Republic's foreign policy in its early years.

## SOURCES OF ADVENTURISM

Since the Islamic Republic's establishment, two factors—revolutionary Islam and Persian nationalism—have driven it into confrontation with its neighbors, with the superpowers, and with a host of governments in the Muslim and broader world. These two sources of adventurism are still strong today in Iran, particularly among key sectors of the elite. Nevertheless, their overall influence on Iran's foreign policy has declined.

## Revolutionary Islam

The Islamic Republic of Iran is a self-professed revolutionary state. Riding high on the initial euphoria after the Islamic revolution, Iranian leaders self-consciously pursued "Islamic" objectives in foreign policy. The clerical regime aided a variety of coreligionists abroad, focusing particular attention on inspiring radical Shi'a groups. Iran, in general, also tried to aid the "dispossessed" against dominant powers, such as the United States and the Soviet Union. Iran rejected the status quo and deliberately incited regional instability—these policies caused it to become a pariah. In general, Tehran forged ties to a variety of Islamist movements and, at times, created them out of whole cloth. Iran supported Islamist revolutionary groups in Iraq, Lebanon, Bahrain, Saudi Arabia, and Kuwait, among other countries. Tehran also denounced any regional governments with pro-Western tendencies as corrupt and un-Islamic, directly challenging their legitimacy.

Iran's revolutionary aspirations did not imply territorial ambitions; its revisionism was related to status, not land. Iran's leadership touted the country's revolutionary credentials to impress sympathizers abroad and, in turn, used its resulting influence abroad to validate its leadership at home.

As time went on, however, the exigencies of day-to-day life made revolutionary ardor a luxury Iran found difficult to afford. Iran's rejection of the status quo and support for regional instability caused its isolation. The war with Iraq forced Tehran to undertake a desperate search for weapons and assistance, even leading it to work in a clandestine manner with its supposed nemeses, Israel and the United States. Years of failure to export revolution successfully—failure that carried a heavy price and led to the regime's isolation—also made Tehran cautious. Iran subsequently avoided massive meddling in Iraq after the Gulf war, despite Baghdad's temporary weakness, and did not make a major play for influence after the Soviet collapse. Tehran also reduced rhetoric critical of pro-Western states, particularly in the Gulf.

Although necessity and foreign policy blunders account for part of Iran's deemphasis of political Islam, much of the explanation for this shift lies in domestic politics. As the heady days of revolution became a distant memory, other concerns rose to the fore. In particular, growing popular disenchantment with the revolutionary regime led to a renewed focus on economic prosperity, and unrest along Iran's borders increased fears of instability at home. The new generation of Iranians taking power is more pragmatic and less committed to revolutionary ideology.[1]

## Persian Nationalism

Since the days of the Shah, Iranian leaders have believed that Iran's size, historical importance, and self-professed cultural superiority merit a significant role for the country in the region. The clerical regime trumpeted nationalism in its war with Iraq to garner domestic support more broadly. In recent years, the regime has also allowed the celebration of the pre-Islamic new year, and many elite members now laud the nationalist hero Mohammed Mosaddeq, despite his anti-Islamic attitude.[2]

Iranian nationalism today, however, is a source of prudence as well as adventurism. In part, nationalism is a reaction to the over-extension of Iran's commitments as dictated by political Islam—a sort of "Come home, Iran," where Iran's own nationally defined (and hence circumscribed) interests take precedence. Hence, it is an "Iran first" movement that rejects unlimited and costly commitments in areas of marginal or indirect importance. Related to this is the secular nature of nationalism, which implies a rejection of the world view espoused by the mullahs that calls on Iran's influence to be identical to that of the broader Muslim religious community.

Nationalism, however, does not mean the end of a difficult Iran. Iran's nationalism is strongly fueled by the history of intervention, manipulation, and exploitation of the country by foreign powers.

---

[1]Mark Gasiorowski, "The Power Struggle in Iran," *Middle East Policy*, Vol. VII, No. 4, October 2000.

[2]Wilfried Buchta, *Who Rules Iran? The Structure of Power in the Islamic Republic* (Washington, DC: Washington Institute for Near East Policy and the Konrad Adenauer Stiftung, 2000), p. 182.

Hence, it defines national independence in terms of following its own path culturally and in foreign policy, of avoiding dependence and extolling self-reliance, and of having a role to play in general. The quest for influence and status will remain an important component of any future Iran.

Iran's nationalism, like its Islamic identity, matters less for territory than for status. Although Iran under the clerical regime has reaffirmed its claim (disputed by the United Arab Emirates [UAE]) to the Greater and Lesser Tunb Islands and expanded its presence on Abu Musa, in general Tehran has not made territorial claims that it might justify through past Persian predominance. Thus, it has avoided claims to parts of Afghanistan, Central Asia, Iraq, and the Gulf that at one time or another were parts of historic Persia.[3]

## SOURCES OF CONSERVATISM

Islam, and to a lesser extent nationalism, initially tended to lead Iran into conflict with its neighbors. Yet Iran's policies have become less confrontational in the last 20 years. Several other forces—Iran's improved geopolitical position, its economic weakness, and its concern for the spread of communal conflict—explain this shift. Iran's security position is difficult even in the best of times. Afghanistan and Iraq, two outright adversaries, host anti-Tehran insurgents. Civil wars and domestic unrest have plagued the Caucasus, Pakistan, and parts of Central Asia. Growing conservatism on the part of Iran's leadership is hardly surprising given this basic instability, Iran's economic weakness, and turmoil at home.

### Geopolitics

Iran's geopolitical environment has changed dramatically since the Islamic revolution. Since that time, the collapse of the Soviet Union,

---

[3]U.S. policy has fed nationalist grievances regarding status. There are those among the nationalists who saw the U.S. policy of containment as posing a direct challenge to Iran's cultural, social, and political well-being. Many nationalists support the government and associated revolutionary causes in part because of this resentment. These and other perspectives are discussed in Hooshang Amirahmadi, ed., *Revisiting Iran's Strategic Significance in the Emerging Regional Order* (New Brunswick, NJ: U.S.-Iran Conference, 1995).

the defeat of Iraq by the U.S.-led coalition and subsequent isolation of Baghdad, and the larger U.S. military presence have altered Iran's basic strategic outlook, making the state and the regime far more secure. As a result, Iran's policies, in the words of Minister of Defense Admiral Ali Shamkhani, are driven in large part by "deterrent defense."[4] With extended maritime borders and seven neighbors by land, Iran has a potentially difficult role in ensuring its own defense.[5] Illegal migration, drug dealing, and smuggling magnify the problem of border security.

There is no clear and present danger to Iran today. The only candidate, Saddam's Iraq, is currently constrained by UN sanctions, international isolation, and its ongoing conflict with the United States and its regional allies. Leaders of all political tendencies in Iran, and the population in general, view the Baath regime with loathing and see Iraq as a long-term threat. Securing Iran against Iraq's threat, however, does not require an immediate military buildup from Iran at this time.

Another feature of Iran's geopolitical situation is the rampant instability that characterizes its immediate neighborhood. A brief survey is sobering:

- Iraq is in danger of fragmenting. The Kurdish north, under U.S. protection, is developing its own institutions, while central authority in Baghdad remains weak.

- Turkey has been fighting an insurgency under a national emergency for the past decade and a half, leading to incursions in neighboring states.

- Pakistan has recently suffered intermittent civil conflict, repeated regime changes, and a military coup.

- Azerbaijan and Armenia have not yet settled their territorial disputes, including those along Iran's border.

---

[4] *Ettela'at International*, January 9, 1997.

[5] This at least is the perception of the Iranian leadership. See Ayatollah Khamene'i's comments to an officers' academy, *Vision of the Islamic Republic of Iran, Network 1* (Tehran, in Persian), October 31, 1999, BBC Summary of World Broadcasts (hereafter cited as BBC) ME/3681 MED/7-8, November 2, 1999.

- Afghanistan's civil war is entering its third decade.

- Tajikistan and its civil war have destabilized several of Tajikistan's neighbors.

Relative to many of its neighbors, Iran is stable. It has a settled historical identity, tested forms of succession, and considerable resources. It is not a failed, or even a failing, state.

With the end of the Soviet Union, the role of Iran in a "new Middle East," defined culturally to include the states of the Caucasus and Central Asia, has become more central. The Soviet Union, and Russia before that, had been a perennial threat to Iran's security and territorial integrity.[6] Its collapse removed a major threat to Iran's security. Moreover, as a crossroads between the Caspian Sea and the Persian Gulf, Iran's position as a transit point and market was enhanced.

While the collapse of the Soviet Union offered opportunity in the north, the relative rise in U.S. power in the Gulf presented a danger and a challenge. Since the 1991 Gulf war, the southern maritime frontiers of Iran have hosted, on average, some 20,000 U.S. troops. Tehran, with reason, sees this presence as aimed at Iran as well as Iraq.

Iran's relative influence with the states of the Gulf Cooperation Council (GCC) also has diminished, in large part because of U.S. efforts. The UAE has repeatedly resisted Iran's territorial claims to several disputed islands in the Persian Gulf, perhaps made bolder by the U.S. defense umbrella. The United States and other Western powers have sold sophisticated equipment to several Gulf states since the end of the Gulf war, leaving Iran—the Gulf's former superpower—a generation or more behind. In its air force today, Iran is both qualitatively and numerically inferior to the Saudis, who had a tiny fraction of Iran's air power when the revolution took place.

The overall geopolitical outlook for Iran, in general, is far more positive than it was in the first decade of the revolution. The situation, however, lacks clarity. As a result, Iranian leaders must take a more

---

[6]Graham Fuller, *The "Center of the Universe"* (Boulder, CO: Westview Press, 1991).

nuanced view of their situation, focusing on the particulars of various countries rather than on a single, coherent threat.

## Ethnicity and Communalism

Both religion and nationalism can, and do, unite Iran's myriad communities, but Iran remains ethnically and religiously diverse. Persians compose 51 percent of Iran's total population. The remainder of Iran's population are Azeri Turk (24 percent),[7] Mazandarani (8 percent), Kurd (7 percent), Arab (3 percent), Baluch (2 percent), Lur (2 percent), and Turkoman (2 percent). Iran is far more unified religiously, roughly 85 percent are Shi'a Muslims, but Sunni Muslims, Christians, Bahais, and Jews also are found in Iran.[8]

While the ethnic minorities differ in their political strength, religious affiliation, and other factors, they have certain elements in common:

- Ethnic minority groups are concentrated mainly in border areas and have ties with ethnic groups or states across the border.

- Many have fostered separatist movements, some of which have briefly led to the establishment of independent states (Kurds in the Mahabad Republic, and the Turks in Azerbaijan, 1945 and 1946).

- The subnational ethnic loyalty competes with and, some would say, overshadows the national (and supranational) identity.

- These groups are largely Sunni (including some Kurds, the Baluch, and the Turkomans), which complicates their relationship with the Shi'a state.

---

[7]Iran's Azeri population, located largely in the northwest but also in Iran's major towns and cities, outnumbers the Azeris in Azerbaijan. Turkish-speaking, the Azeris are Shi'as and, as a result of a long interaction, are a well-integrated linguistic minority. The common religious background has served to facilitate the assimilation of the two separate linguistic groups. Farhad Kazemi, "Ethnicity and the Iranian Peasantry," in Milton Esman and Itamar Rabinovich, eds., *Ethnicity, Pluralism and the State in the Middle East* (Ithaca: Cornell University Press, 1988), p. 213.

[8]Gabriel Ben-Dor, "Ethno-politics and the Middle Eastern State," in Esman and Rabinovich, pp. 85-87. Traditionally, Iran's Shi'a population is given at 90 percent or higher, but this estimate probably undercounts religious minorities. Buchta, *Who Rules Iran?* p. 105.

No group has pursued its drive for autonomy more tenaciously than the Kurds. And none has been more savagely repressed, in part as a warning to other groups.[9] In the years immediately after the revolution, perhaps 20,000 Kurds died as the Islamic Republic brutally suppressed their drive for more autonomy.

As it has with other minorities, Iran has traditionally attempted to assimilate the Kurds into Iranian society but without special nationality status or privileges. Moreover, many Persians look down on Kurds, seeing them as provincial and backward—a sharp contrast to common attitudes toward Azeris and other groups. Iranian officials profess to see no problems with their Kurdish population. This is echoed in statements by some Kurdish leaders, who contrast the Kurds' treatment in Iran favorably with that accorded Kurds in Iraq and Turkey.[10] Kurdish national aspirations are currently limited.

The loyalty of Iran's Kurdish population cannot be taken for granted. They have not forgotten the harsh repression of the early years of the Islamic Republic; their loyalty to the state will depend on how it meets their needs and, to a lesser degree, on regional developments. Moreover, other neighboring states, particularly Iraq, may aid the Kurds as a way of weakening Iran's central government.

Iran's Baluch are also active, though their degree of national consciousness does not approach that of the Kurds. Riots and unrest, along with general lawlessness, have plagued Baluch-populated areas of eastern Iran. Pakistan has allowed Baluch rebels, many of

---

[9]Iranian Kurds number approximately 4 million to 8 million and are approximately 75 percent Sunni and the remainder Shi'a. The Kurdish language is closely related to Persian, with Iranian Kurds viewed as Iranian people with long-standing historical ties.

[10]Foreign Minister Kamal Kharrazi told *IRNA* (Tehran), December 1, 1998: "Like many clans in Iran, the Iranian Kurds have good relations with [the] government of the Islamic Republic of Iran, and peaceful coexistence among all members of the nation created no specific tension," BBC ME/3400 MED/7-8, December 3, 1998. Jalal Talabani, leader of the Iraqi Patriotic Union of Kurdistan (PUK) contrasted the situation in Iran with that in Turkey: "Iran never tried to obliterate the Kurds' identity. There is a province in Iran called Kordestan province. The Iranians name their planes after the provinces in Iran [including Kordestan]." Interview in the Jordanian newspaper *Al-Ahram al-Yawm* (Amman), December 1, 1998, BBC ME/3398 MED/17.

whom are Sunni Islamists, to base themselves across the border in its territory.[11]

The regime's Islamic ideology has often hindered social unity, but pragmatism rather than ideology has increasingly characterized the government's policies toward minorities.[12] In putting forward his vision of an Islamic Republic, Ayatollah Khomeini created apprehension among non-Muslim minorities. As Gabriel Ben-Dor notes, "If an Islamic order is, as defined by its proponents, a total system, it cannot entertain political pluralism, only political separatism."[13] Yet over time, the emphasis was on stability rather than assimilation. As David Menashri observes, "The primary factor shaping the [Islamic Republic] regime's attitude toward the Sunnis has *not* been their ethnic identity or religious affiliation but rather the inherent danger they presented to the stability and territorial integrity of the Islamic Republic."[14]

Yet minority issues remain a perpetual concern to Tehran. Many minority groups live on the periphery of Iran and remain largely together (Kurds in Kurdistan, Baluch in Baluchistan, and so on), creating constant concern about the maintenance of the country's unity.[15] This concern appears well justified, as many minorities have tried to increase their autonomy when the central government has weakened. In addition, many minority groups, including those that

---

[11]Buchta, *Who Rules Iran?* pp. 108-109.

[12]Religious minorities (Jews, Armenians, Bahais, and Zoroastrians) are dependent on the regime and seek its protection. This explains the apparent anomaly that ethnic minorities that are Muslim have been oppressed while religious minorities (with the notable exception of the Bahais) have, by and large, enjoyed a form of tolerance. David Menashri, "Whither Iranian Politics? The Khatami Factor," in Patrick Clawson et al., *Iran Under Khatami: A Political, Economic and Military Assessment*, (Washington, DC: Washington Institute for Near East Policy, 1998), p. 221. However, tolerance is clearly relative. The 1998 show trial of Iranian Jews highlights their precarious position in Iran.

[13]Gabriel Ben-Dor, "Ethno-politics and the Middle Eastern State," in Esman and Rabinovich, p. 90; P.G. Vatikiotis, "Non-Muslims in Muslim Societies," in Esman and Rabinovich, p. 65.

[14]Menashri, in Clawson, p. 218.

[15]Charles MacDonald, "The Kurdish Question in the 1980's," in Esman and Rabinovich, pp. 243-244.

have no political organization, such as the Turkomans, have sought closer ties to their ethnic kinsmen across the borders.[16]

Instability on Iran's borders can affect Iranian society directly. Increasingly, Iran has sought to stabilize its immediate surroundings to prevent major changes that could adversely affect it. As discussed in greater detail below, Iran's ethnic and religious diversity has been a force for caution and moderation in its foreign policy.

## Economics

Ayatollah Khomeini famously said that the revolution was not about "the price of watermelons." Two decades later, however, the Islamic Republic has found that its own nostrums and dicta have little, and diminishing, resonance. As the regime has led the people into war, isolation, and economic decline, it has found the largest part of the population, the young, increasingly alienated. As a result, the revolution *is* increasingly being judged by the price of watermelons. The legitimacy of the Islamic Republic of Iran is now based in large part on what it can deliver economically. This shift is conditioning Iran's attitude to foreign relations. Foreign policy must now buttress the regime economically, even at the price of revolutionary principles.

The basic elements of the economic picture are noted only briefly here. Iran's foreign debts stand at some $14 billion to $17 billion. The "misery index"—the combination of inflation and unemployment—stands at a record high.[17] Inflation rates are between 20 percent and 50 percent. The International Monetary Fund reports that Iran's real GDP per capita remains well below its 1977 level.[18] Some two thirds of Iran's population of 62 million is under 25 years old. Only 14.5 million are now employed. Of the 2 million unemployed, 40 percent are college graduates. As President Khatami put it: "At present our fledgling society wishes to slow down, not eliminate, unemployment figures. It is obliged, therefore, to create 760,000 to

---

[16]Buchta, *Who Rules Iran?* p. 103.

[17]Jahangir Amuzegar. See, for example, his "Khatami and Iranian Economic Policy in the Mid-term," *The Middle East Journal*, vol. 53, no. 4, Autumn 1999, pp. 534-552.

[18]International Monetary Fund, *International Financial Statistics Yearbook* (Washington, DC: International Monetary Fund, 2000).

800,000 jobs a year."[19] The Iranian economy must grow at about 6.7 percent a year—and gain roughly $10 billion in investment a year—to prevent unemployment from increasing.[20] The recent surge in oil prices will buy Iran's leaders some time to maneuver, but this does not eliminate the underlying fundamental problems with Iran's economy. Iran's dependence on oil for some 85 percent of its foreign exchange is as much a handicap as an asset, as it hinders the creation of a competitive and entrepreneurial economy and makes long-term planning difficult due to the fluctuation of oil prices.

These economic problems have taken their toll on Iran's effort to improve its military. Anthony Cordesman writes that Iran's military expenditures in constant dollars were at $8.9 billion after the end of the Iran-Iraq war and have fallen by over half in the latter part of the decade. He notes, "Iran is spending too little to maintain its present force structure to 'recapitalize' it to replace the equipment lost to combat, age, and war, or to modernize its current force structure."[21]

It is hardly surprising that this state of affairs has had serious political repercussions. The demonstrations of some 20,000 youths in July 1999—the largest in the history of the Islamic Republic and a palpable shock to the system—were in large part a reaction to economic problems. These demonstrations were particularly disturbing to the regime, as many participants were from families that had benefited from government programs, including preferred admission to higher education as a result of service in the military or to the government.

The sources of Iran's economic ills are deep. The government and parastatal foundations control most of Iran's economy, stifling initiative and hindering the development of a robust private sector. Oil dominates Iran's economy, to the detriment of other industries. Restrictions on foreign investment, often arbitrary government ac-

---

[19]Excerpts from President Khatami's question-and-answer session with students of the Science and Technology University, December 12, 1999, *Voice of the Islamic Republic of Iran* (Tehran, in Persian), December 13, 1999, BBC ME/3720 MED/6-10, especially p. 9, December 17, 1999.

[20]Amuzegar, "Khatami and Iranian Economic Policy in the Mid-term," pp. 548-550.

[21]Anthony Cordesman, *Iran's Military Forces in Transition* (Westport, CT: Praeger, 1999), p. 45. For a general review, see pp. 41-45.

tions, and general political uncertainty also reduce the prospects for growth.

The remedies to Iran's economic problems are very demanding politically.[22]  A summary of several of the requirements is indicative:

- Greater transparency and respect for the rule of law with regard to property rights.

- A reduction in the government's role in the economy, including privatization of state industrial units, banks, and insurance companies.

- Freedom for the market to determine interest and exchange rates.

- A reduction in the size and scope of the subsidies on food, fuel, medicine, and utilities.

- A reduction in the power of the *bonyads* (parastatal revolutionary foundations), which control much of Iran's economy.[23]  The *bonyads* are not accountable to the public or even to much of the government.  Moreover, they are largely monopolistic and discourage competition in large parts of Iran's economy.

- Encouragement of investment, requiring a revision of tax laws and greater guarantees for investors.

- Acquisition of outside expertise to modernize Iran's oil and gas industries.

- Encouragement of direct foreign investment in Iran's economy.

In general, undertaking these reforms requires good, or at least not hostile, relations with Iran's major trading partners and the world's leading economies.  Regional conflict and a hostile Iranian foreign

---

[22]See Amuzegar, "Khatami and Iranian Economic Policy in the Mid-term," pp. 547-552, and Parviz Aqili, Mussa Ghaninezad, Ali Jahankhani, and Heydar Pourian, "Getting Out of Economic Crisis Needs Courage: We Do Not Have Much Time," *Jameah*, May 9, 1998, p. 7.

[23]Leading *bonyads* include the *Bonyad-e Mostazafan va Janbazan* (Foundation of the Deprived and War Veterans), the *Bonyad-e Alawai*, the *Bonyad-e Shahid* (Martyrs' Foundation), the *Bonyad-e Maskan* (Housing Foundation), the *Bonyad-e 15th Khordad*, the Imam Khomeini Relief and Aid Organization, and the *Jihad-e Sazandeghi* (Reconstruction Crusade).

policy will hinder investment, prevent the return of expertise to Iran, and make ties to the international market (both financial and trade) a source of instability rather than prosperity.

A lukewarm consensus on the need for reform exists in Iran, but its shape remains fuzzy. An improved economic performance—currently taking place due to the higher price of oil in the last year—might buy the regime time and so make substantial political reforms unnecessary. Hence, even Khatami's conservative opponents are prepared to give him a certain amount of leeway to see if he can produce results and to blame him if he cannot. Nevertheless, vested interests will likely stop many necessary measures from being undertaken. The clerical regime (so far) is unwilling to undertake the requisite measures because of the impact on its core constituency, the bazaar, which opposes privatization, and the hard-liners, bully boys, enforcers, and gangsters (for example, *Ansar-e Hezballah*) on which it depends. Ideological concerns also inhibit reform. Many among the old guard believe that market-friendly reforms will disadvantage Iran's poor. Differences exist on the priority to be attached to social justice policies, such as subsidies to various businesses, and the level of overall government spending and taxation.

## IMPACT ON IRAN'S FOREIGN POLICY

The foreign policy implications of revolutionary Islam, geopolitics, nationalism, ethnicity, and economics differ considerably. Moreover, these concepts are vague enough that, when applied to specific policies, their implications are not clear. Nevertheless, Table 2.1 presents notional and brief descriptions of core foreign policy areas. It suggests how the source in question (that is to say, Islam, economics, and so on) *should* affect policy and then notes Iran's actual policies. When the impact is not clear, the box is blank. The purpose is to compare the different inputs and note their relative strength.

As the table suggests, Iran's actual policies do not square neatly with any of the main drivers identified. Rather, a combination of factors, which often rise and fall in importance, has affected Iran's actual policies. Ethnicity and economics, however, dominate Iran's behavior in several key areas. Relations with the United States are one of the few exceptions where ideology and nationalism appear to play a greater role.

## Table 2.1
### Drivers of Iran's Foreign Policy Compared

| Selected Issue | Revolutionary Islam | Geopolitics | Nationalism | Ethnicity | Economics | Actual Policy |
|---|---|---|---|---|---|---|
| Defense spending level | — | Low | High | — | Low | Low |
| Ties to revolutionary movements | Strong ties to Muslim groups, particularly Shi'a | Ties to groups in key states, such as Iraq | Ties to groups in the Gulf region, Central Asia, and other historical areas of interest | Reject most ties; strong ties to governments | Reject most ties that might hinder trade or stability | Cautious ties to various religious groups; decline in support in recent years |
| Relations with the Gulf states | Competition and rejection of legitimacy | Attempt to decrease U.S. influence | Seek recognition of Iran's leadership | Avoid policies that might anger Arab Iranians | Seek close ties to gain goodwill of West, improve oil cooperation | Steady rapprochement |
| Relations with Central Asia and the Caucasus | Support for religious groups | Balance Azerbaijan (and Turkey) with Armenia | Seek influence in Tajikistan, other Persian areas | Strong ties to governments to prevent irredentism | Pursue close economic ties | Pursue economic ties; good relations with regional governments |
| Relations with the United States | Reject ties | Recognize U.S. power; avoid confrontation; minimize U.S. influence | Reject ties, particularly if perceived as subordinate | — | Seek good relations with Washington | Continued resistance to normalization |

# Chapter Three

# SECURITY DECISIONMAKING IN IRAN

The decisionmaking process in Iran can be, and often is, bewildering in its complexity. The large number of institutions, the important roles of nongovernment actors, overlapping institutional structures, the importance of personal ties, and lack of a clear division of labor among security ministries often lead to conflicting policies and uncertain implementation.

Although planning for Iran's national security is the constitutional task of the *Artesh* and the mandate of Iran's other security organizations, Iran does not have a single national security approach, or program of action. Policy outcomes are usually products of compromises reached by the security community itself and its political masters.

This chapter provides an overview of decisionmaking in Iran, focusing on the role—and limits—played by Iran's security institutions. It discusses the style of decisionmaking, the formal and informal mechanisms, and the means the military uses to influence policy.

## DECISIONMAKING STYLE: CONSENSUS WITHIN COMPLEXITY

Any attempt to capture a nation's decisionmaking process is bound to simplify. That said, Iran's decisionmaking is characterized by two competing trends. The complexity and apparent chaos of the Iranian system is marked, particularly to the outsider. The large number of institutional and noninstitutional actors, family ties, personal relationships, overlapping institutional authority, and mixture of religion and politics all contrive to make it difficult to identify who has a say on what issue. Often many voices are heard, and similar issues often involve different actors within the system.[1]

This complexity is balanced, however, by a cultural and procedural emphasis on consensus. Although debates in Iran are often fierce, major decisions seldom go forward without at least a tacit consensus among the elite. At the highest levels, regime figures may constantly scheme against one another, but they seldom directly challenge each other, preferring instead to horse trade and compromise and thus, ironically, to work together. Moreover, elites seem to be governed by a set of informal rules known to the players, if not to outsiders. Elites, for example, can monitor meetings, Friday prayer sessions, and internal pronouncements to judge who is involved with which decisions.

Indeed, the system requires compromise in order to avoid paralysis. With so many input points into decisionmaking, and so many overlapping or parallel institutions, cooperation is necessary to accomplish even the most basic functions of government.[2]

The apparent chaos that characterizes Iran's institutions often gives the impression that important players act without oversight. This impression is usually false. To preserve the consensus, few actors dare conduct important operations without at least tacit approval of the senior leadership. Particularly at lower levels, individuals hesitate to make decisions without authorization from above. Because of the emphasis on consensus, "rogue operations" by security officials are generally not likely.

Iran's institutional structure reinforces oversight, or at least knowledge, of security operations. Since the introduction of constitutional reforms in 1989, the command and control of the *Faqih*, or Supreme Leader, have been exercised in an elaborate interlocking pattern in which no single organ or individual could hold the upper hand or act independently of the political leadership. For almost all operations,

---

[1]Buchta, *Who Rules Iran?* p. xi.

[2]Wilfried Buchta makes this point about the need for cooperation between the Supreme Leader and the President, but it applies to Iranian politics more broadly. Buchta, *Who Rules Iran?* p. 4.

the Ministry of Intelligence and Security (MOIS) and the covert elements of the IRGC report to at least a subset of the Supreme Council for National Security (SCNS), including the President, the Supreme Religious Leader, and the Minister of Intelligence.[3]  Informal networks provide even more information.  Leaders are likely to be at least aware of important decisions and operations through their personal networks.

This mix of complexity and consensus makes predicting decisionmaking difficult.  While there is a formal system for decisionmaking, it is often ignored or bypassed.  Individuals are constantly tempted to ignore the system, particularly if it is easier to gain a consensus that way.  Prediction is made even more difficult because there are many access points into Iranian decisionmaking.  Major decisions are influenced by leading merchants, religious figures (both affiliated with and opposed to the regime), political loyalists of all stripes, and others, who use their economic, social, and ideological power to influence political decisions.

Iranian decisionmaking often is characterized by broad agreement that is tempered by constant renegotiation and haphazard execution. As a result, Iran's security policy often follows different, if usually complementary, lines.  Major policies, such as confrontation with the United States or support for radicals abroad, require consensus among the regime's leadership, but implementation of these agreed-on policies may vary widely.

The result is often a constant back-and-forth process.  Different institutions that are not equally enthusiastic about a change may implement policies inconsistently or unevenly, leading to mixed signals in Iran's foreign policy.  In addition, policy slippage regularly occurs due to the constant renegotiation of controversial issues.

## Formal Decisionmaking Structures

On paper, Iran has a coherent structure for security decisionmaking. The President exercises considerable day-to-day authority, and he controls budget planning, which is essential for incorporating mili-

---

[3]Cordesman, *Iran's Military Forces in Transition*, p. 34.

tary priorities into overall grand strategy. The Supreme Leader (*Faqih*), however, is the most important official. Under article 110 of the 1979 constitution, the Supreme Leader retains the constitutional right to declare war and call for general troop mobilization. He is also the supreme commander of both the IRGC and the *Artesh*.[4]

Although the *Faqih* is the commander-in-chief of the armed forces, he disposes of his responsibilities toward the defense establishment not through any direct chain of command. According to the formal system, the *Faqih* works through other bodies in exercising his control.

Today, the SCNS, chaired by the President, is the key national defense and security assessment body. Representatives of the *Artesh*, the IRGC, other security agencies, and the *Faqih* sit on the council. This forum discusses, calculates, and formulates responses to threats to national security. During the Afghan crisis in 1998, for instance, the SCNS evaluated the threat and plotted a response.[5] The response may not have been to the liking of some conservative elements in the IRGC and the broader political establishment (who would have liked a military confrontation with the Taliban in Afghanistan), but the predominant line—escalation without risk of war—championed by the *Artesh* and several IRGC commanders prevailed. In the end, and not for the first time, the Supreme Leader endorsed the recommendations of the SCNS on the handling of the Afghan crisis and did not order a general troop mobilization.

The *Faqih*, however, exercises tremendous indirect control. The office of the *Faqih* enjoys residual prestige from its association with the Imam. The *Faqih* relies on an elaborate system of interconnected directorships, whereby his representatives sit on decisionmaking bodies in various elements of the defense establishment. The *Faqih* does not often play a role in the day-to-day concerns but guides overall direction through his representatives. An estimated 2,000 Islamic "commissars" work under the Supreme Leader's direction.[6]

---

[4]He receives advice on national security and defense matters from two military officers in his office, and he receives reports on foreign affairs from a foreign affairs advisor, currently the former Foreign Minister Ali Akbar Velayati.

[5]Private conversations with political figures.

[6]Buchta, *Who Rules Iran?* pp. 3 and 48.

Islamization is perhaps the most singularly important dimension that the Islamists have added to the former Imperial structures, including the armed services. An Ideological-political Directorate is present at all levels of the services. Its members, usually middle-ranking clerics, sit in on many meetings, eat with officers, encourage them to pray together, and hold discussion meetings. The Ideological-political Directorate is therefore influential in setting the atmosphere in military corridors and in barracks. The directorate is also influential in decisions about promotions, special assignments, and so on. Few senior officers are promoted on the basis of military merit alone. Rather, they must have revolutionary credentials and political connections.[7]

## Key Informal Mechanisms

Family, kinship, educational affiliations, and support from various clerical personalities and factions play a central role in military politics in general, for both the IRGC and the *Artesh*. Personal networks are almost always stronger than institutional power.[8] Important individuals have relatives, friends, and protégés in related ministries. Many also share a revolutionary background, having worked together against the Shah in the Islamic underground or sharing time in the Shah's jails. Many come from the same Islamic school or seminar. For example, many of the top cadre in the MOIS come from the Madrase-ye Haqqani, a leading theological school in Qom.[9] As Wilfried Buchta argues, "The Iranian government's successful function is often at the mercy of these informal networks."[10]

---

[7]For example, Rear Admiral Ali Shamkhani came from the ranks of the IRGC, drew closer to then-President Hashemi Rafsanjani's camp in the early 1990s, and is now one of the most important players in the military field as a prominent member of Khatami's cabinet. Also, Air Force Commander Brigadier Habib Baqai comes with impeccable politico-religious credentials.

[8]Examples of the importance of personal relationships are too numerous to count in recent Iranian history. Foreign Minister Kamal Kharrazi's nephew is his deputy; Brigadier General Hejazi, the commander of the *Basij*, has a son who helps run the office of Ayatollah Khamene'i; Ayatollah Kadivar, a cleric recently released from jail, is the brother-in-law of Minister of Culture and Islamic Guidance Ataollah Mohajerani, whose wife is a member of parliament.

[9]Buchta, *Who Rules Iran?* p. 166.

[10]Buchta, *Who Rules Iran?* p. 7.

The idiosyncratic structure of Iran's national security apparatus contributes to the informal power of selected officials. Ties to political factions enable military officials to express their views outside the chain of command. Military commanders often exchange views when the *Faqih* invites them to meet him or his representatives.

Both family ties and shared experience are important to advancement in the IRGC. Many IRGC commanders come from religious families and have married into other religious families. These networks, which operate on weekends, before and after Friday prayers, and through family gatherings and events (births, marriages, deaths, funerals, and so on), provide informal but effective means of communication among commanders and among individuals of the political class as well. The IRGC high command still consists of many of the officers who served in the war or who were around from the early days of the revolution. In the regular forces—where much of the recruitment is still done through conscription and where officer material goes through the military academy and its training wing—such ties seem less important.

An obvious implication of these informal networks is that institutions in Iran are weak. Understanding decisionmaking power in Iran thus requires understanding not just an individual's place on an organization chart, but also his ties to other leaders. These cross-cutting relations, in turn, hinder coherent organizational identities and agendas.

## THE IMPLICATIONS OF MULTIPLE INSTITUTIONS

Iran's institutions overlap tremendously, both on paper and in reality. The IRGC and the *Artesh* have duplicate services, further confused by overlap with Iran's intelligence and cultural bodies. Moreover, their missions overlap in practice; for example, separating the defense of the revolution (the IRGC's raison d'être) from the defense of Iran's borders is often impossible.

Iran's security organizations are numerous, often overlap, and have an uncertain command and control structure. On paper, the President would seem to exercise tremendous oversight. The Supreme Leader has influence in both the formal governmental security organizations (the regular army and the intelligence and interior ministries) and in the revolutionary organizations, such as the IRGC and the paramilitary militia known as the *Basij*. The President, on the other hand, exercises only indirect influence over the revolutionary organizations through the Ministry of Defense.

The organization chart, however, is misleading. It is confusing on paper, but the reality is far more complex. The many informal mechanisms, and the importance of individual ties, make it difficult to square ostensible responsibilities with real ones.

Overlapping duties, however, are deliberate, despite their inefficiency. Infighting among regime members has led to competing multiple centers of power in general; the military's multiple centers are thus merely a reflection of the power structure in general. The overlapping nature of the security institutions has several benefits for regime stability, but it often makes a coherent security policy far more difficult. When multiple institutions have a security role, a successful military takeover of power becomes far more difficult.[11] Thus, potential coup plotters must be sure of the loyalty, or at least the passivity, of the IRGC, the *Artesh*, the intelligence services, and even the *Basij* if they are to succeed. Similarly, it is highly likely that the conservative forces in the regime would be able to call on at least some elements of Iran's security establishment to aid their cause; reformers can at best hope for passivity.

## How Influence Is Expressed

The influence of Iran's security institutions is felt in a defused way and tends to be quite issue specific. They exercise their muscle in such forums as the SNSC, at advisory meetings with the Supreme Leader and the presidential office, and through their discussions with the Majles' foreign and security committees. All the security institutions also use their informal access, through family and religious ties and so on, to influence decisionmaking.

---

[11]James Quinlivan, "Coup Proofing: Its Practice and Consequences in the Middle East," *International Security*, vol. 24, no. 2, Fall 1999, pp. 131-165.

The security institutions also exploit their control over information to influence debate, particularly among elites. This ability to influence agendas is strong when it comes to threats from insurgent groups, such as the *Mujahedin-e Khalq* Organization (MKO), and more technical military issues, such as the capabilities of the forces of neighboring states. However, on broader security issues, such as the disposition of the Taliban or the threat posed by Iraq, their control over information is limited.

The *Artesh*'s main forum is the SCNS, which is charged with overseeing all national security matters. However, by virtue of having a seat at the cabinet table, the *Artesh* also expresses its opinions in cabinet discussions of foreign affairs, the national budget, procurement, allocation of resources, and so on. The *Artesh* also has informal access to the Supreme Leader's office, but it does not seem to regard this as being a decisive arena of influence.

The IRGC, on the other hand, routinely exploits its access to the Supreme Leader's office, volunteers advice on national and foreign policy matters to the Leader and his key staff, and actively aims to influence policy and debate on security issues. The IRGC also exercises its influence through contact with conservative-leaning clergy in Qom, who have considerable influence in the judiciary, the Interior Ministry, the Expediency Council, and the Council of Guardians. It further exercises its influence through its organizational links to and leadership of the *Basij*. Commonly, IRGC leaders address Friday prayers, at which they discuss a wide range of policy matters. Increasingly, the IRGC, or leadership groups within it, issues statements and also warnings to the President and his allies on national security issues. By contrast, the *Artesh* simply does not conduct itself in this fashion.

## TRENDS IN OVERALL INFLUENCE

The *Artesh*'s star has been rising in recent years even though the IRGC enjoys better access to regime elites, particularly the Supreme Leader. In part this rise is due to the concurrent rise of the Khatami agenda: As the more pragmatic agenda initiated by Rafsanjani and expanded by Khatami has come to dominate Iran's foreign policy, so too has the influence enjoyed by the more pragmatic *Artesh*. The increase in focus on economics and stability squares with the *Artesh*'s more defensive agenda. The IRGC, in contrast, is increasingly viewed as an overtly ideological institution that cannot be trusted for impartial advice on national security matters.

The IRGC's influence, however, remains considerable when domestic affairs and national security mix. This is particularly true for efforts to safeguard the revolution against the MKO or other internal opponents, even though assassinations or other covert actions abroad often have considerable negative consequences.

The question of how much influence the military has, and how it exercises this influence, is bound up in the nature of the Iranian state itself. Iran is unusual in the Middle East for the limited role that the military plays in national political life and in the conduct of the country's foreign policy. The *Artesh* and the IRGC offer expertise at the discussion level of strategic issues and assessment of potential tensions for the political leadership. Far more than do Western militaries, they also try to influence the national debate. However, they do not call the shots and are often overruled by civilian officials. Civilian control, while hardly complete, remains dominant and prevents the military from behaving as a rogue actor.

# Chapter Four

# MAJOR SECURITY INSTITUTIONS AND THEIR COMPOSITION

Myriad individuals, institutions, and organizations play important foreign policy roles in Iran. For issues of security policy—the focus of this report—several organizations are particularly important, including the intelligence services, the Islamic Revolutionary Guard Corps (IRGC) and the paramilitary militia known as the *Basij*, and the regular armed forces, or *Artesh*.

Recognizing the role of the Iranian armed forces and security services is critical to understanding Iran's security policy. These institutions will respond to the challenges of the 21st century, be it the return of Iraq as a major regional power, a powerful Turkish-Israeli axis, possible domestic turmoil in the southern Gulf states, a meltdown in Afghanistan, or other core concerns. Moreover, they must do so with a relatively limited budget (of at most $5 billion a year), inferior military equipment (relative to that of other regional powers), and a divided political elite whose only priority and goal might be survival. These organizations, their relative power, and their institutional biases are discussed below.

## THE INTELLIGENCE SERVICES

Iran's intelligence services play an active role in its foreign policy, particularly with regard to efforts to suppress Iranian dissidents and to support coreligionists abroad. Open information on Iran's leading intelligence organization, the Ministry of Intelligence and Security

(MOIS), is extremely limited—this report offers at best a limited description of the MOIS's goals and actions.

Many MOIS functions are tied to defending the regime and ensuring the strength of the government, and to protecting Iran's interests abroad. Under the constitution, the MOIS gathers and assesses information and, more important, acts against conspiracies endangering the Islamic Republic. The MOIS, controlled by Khatami's allies, has steadily purged hard-liners since Khatami's election in 1997.[1]

## IRAN'S TWO MILITARIES

Iran's military forces are the heart of Iran's security institutions. The Islamic Republic began its life with two, often competing, military forces, which maintain their separate existences to this day.

Iran's regular military, the *Artesh*, stood aside during the revolutionary turmoil that overwhelmed the Shah.[2] The officer corps soon was decimated through desertion, forced retirement, and execution at the hands of the overzealous revolutionary courts.[3] Before long, Iran's new political masters set about changing many of the organizational structures of the regular armed forces. The regime implemented a massive campaign of Islamization of the armed forces, conducted through the newly established Ideological-political Directorate. Although this did not instill revolutionary ardor into the *Artesh*, it did stamp out any potential counterrevolutionary sentiment and ensured that the armed forces remained responsible to the political leadership. Despite having cowed the *Artesh*, the clerical regime felt the need to create is own armed forces to ensure internal stability and, over time, act as a major force in the war with

---

[1]Gasiorowski, "The Power Struggle in Iran."

[2]While the Imperial armed forces of the Shah were highly trained and enjoyed the benefits of a motivated, professional, and loyal officer corps, the bulk of the army consisted of a conscripted force that had little interest in defending the Pahlavi regime against internal enemies. So, when the crunch came and the revolution gathered pace, the soldiers were on the street, but their commanders were always in doubt about their loyalty. For a fascinating account, see General Robert E. Huyser, *Mission to Tehran* (London: Andre Deutsch, 1986).

[3]Buchta estimates that 45 percent of Iran's officer corps was purged between 1980 and 1986. Buchta, *Who Rules Iran?* p. 68.

Iraq.  The result was two militaries, the regular military and the Islamic Revolutionary Guard Corps (IRGC), or *Sepah-e Pasdaran.*

## The Emergence of an Islamized Military

From the start, the link between internal security and the armed forces was tight.  The *Artesh* did not pose a serious challenge to the new order (relegating such events as the Nowjeh air force coup attempt of July 1980 to a historical footnote).  The challenge, when it did come, was from leftist groups and ethnic uprisings, particularly the Kurds but also the Turkomans, the Baluchi, and some Azeris.[4]

This challenge spawned the IRGC, which is today one of the main security pillars of the Islamic Republic.  The IRGC began as a modest force of about 10,000 men dedicated to returning order to the country, dampening counterrevolutionary trends among the regular armed forces, and countering the growing influence of largely leftist revolutionary armed groups such as the *Fedayeen, Mujahedin-e Khalq* Organization (MKO), *Peykar, Komleh,* Kurdish *Peshmerga,* and so on.  Although it is almost impossible to be precise, the *Fedayeen* and the MKO may have had as many as 10,000 fully armed volunteers each.  So, the IRGC at its inception was not a dominant military force.  Indeed, many of its initial activities had more to do with guarding key personnel of the new regime and with keeping public order than with fighting to defend the new order.  Its size, power, and influence steadily expanded as the regime tried to consolidate its power.[5]

The Iraqi invasion of Iran in September 1980 forced Iran's political and military leadership to face up to the command and structural problems of having two very different armed forces existing in parallel.  The war, more than any other event, placed the structuring of the Iranian armed forces and the state's coercive machinery on the national agenda.

---

[4]Dilip Hiro, *Iran Under the Ayatollahs* (London: Routledge and Keegan Paul, 1995).

[5]Shaul Bakhash, *The Reign of the Ayatollahs: Iran and the Islamic Revolution* (London: I.B. Tauris, 1985).

One direct impact of the war was to force the regime to reorganize the IRGC into proper military units, which was accomplished by late 1981.[6] Another direct by-product of the war was the rapid expansion of the IRGC from 10,000 troops in 1980 to around 50,000 by the beginning of 1982.[7] The force as a whole experienced dramatic expansion throughout the war years, from 150,000 in 1983, to 250,000 in 1985, and to 450,000 in 1987.

A third, structural change introduced in the early 1980s was the creation of an Operational Area Command (in 1982) and a joint Command Council, which brought the commanders of the IRGC in direct and regular contact with their counterparts in the regular armed forces. By now, the IRGC also enjoyed representation and an influential voice in the highest military decisionmaking body, the Supreme Defense Council.

While the regular armed forces had suffered numerous purges and forced retirements in the 1980s, the IRGC flourished under a group of commanders who not only had very close links with the clerical establishment but were also closely allied with one another. The relationships among these key individuals—Mohsen Rafiqdoust, Mohsen Rezai, Yahya Rahim Safavi, Ali Shamkhani, and Alireza Afshar—were reinforced by a low circulation of senior personnel in the IRGC in the 1980s, ensuring that the IRGC could pursue its interests coherently and systematically.[8] These individuals have continued their relationships as they have gone on to other important economic and political positions in the Islamic Republic. Such continuity in leadership also allowed the IRGC's main strategists to be permanently present at the highest levels in both governmental and clerical circles, giving the IRGC the capacity to carve a niche for itself as not just the defender of the revolutionary order but also a guardian of the Islamic state's borders and territory. In contrast, regular army officials remained stigmatized by their association with the Shah and their lack of revolutionary credentials.

---

[6]Anthony H. Cordesman and Abraham R. Wagner, *The Lessons of Modern War—Volume II: The Iran-Iraq War* (Boulder, CO: Westview Press, 1990).

[7]International Institute for Strategic Studies, *The Military Balance* (various years); Jaffee Center for Strategic Studies, *The Middle East Military Balance* (various years).

[8]Sepehr Zabih, *The Iranian Military in Revolution and War* (London: Routledge, 1988).

In the early 1980s, elements from the new leadership of the *Artesh* pushed for the professionalization of the IRGC and for closer command structures with this force.  Senior officers, such as then-colonels Ali Shirazi (who later became Ayatollah Khomeini's representative on the Supreme Defense Council) and Qasemali Zahirnejad (later to become Chief of Staff), were among those arguing in favor of the mechanization of the IRGC and closer integration of logistical and support systems of the two forces.[9]

The moves to rationalize the military structures and command systems continued throughout the 1980s, partly as a response to the growing importance of the IRGC in the war and partly due to the regular armed forces' desire to transform the IRGC into a more professional fighting machine.  In the early days of the fighting, the *Artesh* assumed the lion's share of the burden for the war.  Over time, the IRGC's role in the new order became so significant that it was given a whole new administrative machinery, its own ministry, in 1982, with Mohsen Rafiqdoust as its first minister. This IRGC Ministry mirrored the Defense Ministry, and the IRGC, by virtue of having a ministry, acquired a powerful voice at the cabinet table and in other central governmental agencies.  The evolution of the IRGC into a full fighting machine was completed fewer than three years later, in 1985, when, on a direct order from Ayatollah Khomeini, the IRGC was given the task of setting up its own army, navy, and air force units.  It was also given control over Iran's surface-to-surface missile (SSM) force and right of first refusal on Iran's increasingly scarce military hardware, which includes Iraqi armor now being acquired at the front.[10]  The IRGC also forged its own military-to-military ties to a number of Iran's allies, including Syria, Pakistan, and the Sudan.[11]

## The Legacy of the Iran-Iraq War

The war with Iraq left a strong imprint on Iranian defense thinking, even among the clerical elite.  The war cost between 350,000 and 400,000 Iranian lives, and the two countries have still not signed a

---

[9]Zabih, *The Iranian Military in Revolution and War.*

[10]Shahram Chubin and Charles Tripp, *Iran and Iraq at War* (London: I.B. Tauris, 1988).

[11]Buchta, *Who Rules Iran?* p. 68.

peace treaty ending the conflict.  The failure of Iran to translate its ideological fervor into military success undermined the idea that military power counted for little, that professional military forces were unnecessary, that revolutionary ardor mattered more than professionalism, and that military hardware was unimportant.  The war underscored the importance of access to technology, professional competence, regular exercises, and deterrence.

The war also made self-reliance in defense a cardinal goal.  The war saw the end of the supply of arms from the United States and the need to shift from Western to Eastern suppliers for the air force.  Iran also built up its domestic defense industries.  In addition, the lack of spares for U.S.-supplied aircraft, together with the initiation of missile attacks by Iraq from 1983, culminating in the 1988 "war of the cities," saw a shift to missiles *instead* of aircraft.

## IRAN'S MILITARY FORCES AFTER THE IRAN-IRAQ WAR

After the end of the war, and particularly after the election victory of President Rafsanjani in 1989, a major overhaul of the Iranian security establishment began.  Rafsanjani took steps to rationalize the regular armed forces.[12]  At the same time, the process of professionalization and institutionalization of the IRGC began.  Thus, between August 1988 and September 1988, the IRGC's ground forces were reorganized into 21 infantry divisions, 15 independent infantry brigades, 21 air defense brigades, three engineering divisions, and 42 armored, artillery, and chemical defense brigades.  The IRGC was given new uniforms, and, in September 1991, 21 new military ranks (divided along four categories of soldiers, fighters, officers, and commandants) were created, from private to general.

---

[12]The first steps of the reforms, however, were being taken even before the implementation of the UN-brokered cease-fire in July 1988, as the creation in June 1988 of a joint Armed Forces General Staff illustrates.  It was then that Ayatollah Khomeini took the unusual step of placing Rafsanjani as the acting commander in chief. A month later, Iran had accepted Security Council Resolution 598.  Anoushiravan Ehteshami, *After Khomeini: The Iranian Second Republic* (London: Routledge, 1995).

Another step in the reform process was the establishment in 1989 of an overhauled defense-related structure, to be known as the Ministry of Defense and Armed Forces Logistics (MODAFL). This new ministry, headed by Akbar Torkan, a civilian and a former head of the defense industries establishment, effectively curtailed the institutional autonomy of the IRGC and brought it under the overall defense umbrella. With this act, the IRGC Ministry was scrapped, and its command structures were brought within the new MODAFL. Insofar as the new structure placed restrictions on the operational autonomy of the IRGC, it was a victory for not only the pragmatists over the revolutionaries, but also the *Artesh*. The next big step was the expansion of the joint staff office, which was hastily created in 1988, into a more enduring structure. The new single office of the joint chiefs of staff, the General Command of the Armed Forces Joint Staffs, was set up in early 1992, headed by Hassan Firouzabadi, a prominent IRGC figure.[13] These structural reforms, accompanied by major new arms procurements for the *Artesh*, also signaled the post-Khomeini leadership's interest in allowing the power pendulum to swing back toward the regular armed forces.

The *Artesh*'s power further grew in 1998 in response to the crisis in Afghanistan. Khamene'i created the position of Supreme Commander for the regular military, a position that the IRGC had but the *Artesh* did not—its services reported separately rather than to one individual. This increased both the efficiency and the bureaucratic clout of the regular armed forces. The fact that Khamene'i issued this directive also suggests that the revolutionary leadership's suspicion of the military had declined.[14]

Since these reforms were enacted, the defense establishment has demonstrated the growing integration of its various elements through regular military exercises, on land and offshore as well. Units from the IRGC and the *Artesh* have been seen working quite closely in these exercises, sharing command and systems. The navies of the two institutions are better integrated than are their land and air forces. Nevertheless, considerable problems remain. The two militaries do not have a coherent way of dividing up arms Iran

---

[13]Buchta, *Who Rules Iran?* p. 147.

[14]Buchta, *Who Rules Iran?* p. 147.

procures abroad or develops at home. Friction is acute in the ground and air forces, and integration in these services is fitful at best.

## THE *BASIJ*

Another element of the post-revolution Iranian defense establishment is the *Basij*, the large and initially highly motivated group of volunteers who were trained by the IRGC and who often made the first wave of Iranian offensives against Iraq. In essence, the *Basij* had two functions: first, to fight the domestic enemies of the revolution as the regime's urban shock troops; and second, to provide the large pool of reservists for front-line operations against Iraq.

In the 1980s, the *Basij* was required to fulfill both these functions simultaneously. During the war with Iraq, the *Basij*'s numbers fluctuated between 100,000 and 500,000, depending on the regime's war needs, but its role and presence in military campaigns were never questioned. Today, the *Basij*'s numbers stand at around 100,000, but the *Basij* reserve force is estimated to be around 1 million—most of whom have received some military training or served at the war fronts in the 1980s.

The end of the war and the demobilization of hundreds of thousands of young men, many of whom were volunteer *Basij*, caused an immediate headache for the government. The question was how to appease these dedicated supporters and meet their material needs while also tackling the structural problems of the economy—which required reducing subsidies and other measures that populist regimes traditionally use to sustain key constituencies.

Two responses were adopted with vigor. One policy was to use the *Basij* for nonmilitary national reconstruction work, particularly relevant during the Rafsanjani administration's first five-year development plan, when much state investment concentrated on capital projects, the improvement of the country's infrastructure, and the rebuilding of the war-damaged regions. Engaging the *Basij* with reconstruction priorities provided the men with an income and a role serving the revolution as well.

The second policy initiated direct *Basij* intervention in society. The youth who had gathered around the *Basij* in the 1980s were mobilized in the 1990s as the principle force responsible for upholding Islamic norms in society. Some *Basij* were enrolled in the *Ansar-e Velayat*, a paramilitary group that helps the regime control major urban areas. This was a rather convenient solution to a serious problem facing the Islamic elite—how to reweave the *Basij* back into a peacetime institutional framework cost effectively while also including it in a core function of the Islamic state.

With each passing year, the *Basij* becomes less of a military factor, let alone an active player. The *Basij* is now rarely seen as the third military pillar, as it was during the Iran-Iraq war. The *Artesh* in particular has little time for the *Basij*. Even the IRGC, which once relied heavily on the *Basij*, no longer views it as important, largely because it does not meet the IRGC's level of professionalism. However, the IRGC still encourages the *Basij* to participate in maneuvers and other limited forms of cooperation.

Yet the *Basij* still seeks some external security role. The *Basij* leaders derive a great deal of prestige and legitimacy from their role as a military factor and clearly do not want to lose this status. Most *Basij* leaders do not want to lose their revolutionary edge and are committed to following the IRGC's instructions on training and other operational procedures. However, for *Basij* leaders, official positions are much more important than military training. The relationship between the IRGC and the *Basij* leadership is a close one, driven as it is by family ties, political association, and war experience.

## OTHER PARAMILITARY GROUPS AND SECURITY PLAYERS

Numerous other actors also play a role in formulating and implementing Iran's security policy. These include paramilitary groups, parastatal organizations, and cultural organizations. Also important are several religious leaders, including many not affiliated with the regime, who have a significant following outside of Iran. A complete listing of these groups is beyond the scope of this study. However, several of the more important ones are noted below.

The *Ansar-e Hezbollah* is a paramilitary force of little or no military value but useful for defending the revolutionary order against an array of its critics. In essence, the *Ansar* is a response to the rapid social liberalization that has been going on in the 1990s. The *Ansar* members are the thugs upon whom the right relies to intimidate society.

Factionalism, a constant feature of the republican regime, has caused Iran's top leaders to recruit their own armed guards, who have in the past been deployed against rivals. The most public instances of such deployments were those between Ayatollah Khomeini and Ayatollah Shariatmadari in the early 1980s and between Khomeini and Ayatollah Montazeri in the late 1980s.

The parastatal organizations, the *bonyads,* also play a role in foreign policy.[15] Many *bonyad* leaders have ties to the security institutions. The archetypal example is the former head of the *Bonyad-e Mostazafan,* Mohsen Rafiqdoust, who went from being Khomeini's driver to assuming a leading IRGC position before heading the *Bonyad-e Mostazafan.* Huge sums are transferred from the *bonyads,* particularly the *Bonyad-e Mostazafan,* to the Supreme Leader. This gives him considerable autonomy and the ability to exercise policy without support from other Iranian institutions. The *bonyads* at times act without the formal support of all of Iran's policy makers. The *Bonyad-e 15$^{th}$ Khordad* established, and raised, the bounty on Salman Rushdie, despite efforts by Khatami to annul the edict calling for his death, effectively hindering Iran's rapprochement with Europe. Many Iranians believe that the *bonyads* provide support to the Lebanese Hezballah, but hard evidence is lacking. In 1993, however, Hezballah leaders claimed that the *Jihad al-Binaa* would provide $8.7 million to repair houses damaged by Israeli strikes. The *Bonyad-e Shahid* also provides stipends to families of martyrs.[16]

Various cultural and information agencies play an important role in Iran's foreign policy. Cultural bureaus acting out of embassies often represent the Supreme Leader, placing their activities outside the formal control of Iran's Foreign Ministry. These institutions provide financial support to friendly Muslim movements and proselytize.[17] The Islamic Propagation Organization (IPO) also devotes some re-

---

[15]The *Jihad-e Sazandeghi* (Reconstruction Crusade) is also technically part of the security forces, as it is allowed, in emergencies, to apply force to ensure order in rural areas. Buchta, *Who Rules Iran?* p. 65.

[16]Hala Jaber, *Hezballah: Born with a Vengeance* (London: Fourth Estate, 1997), p. 124.

[17]Buchta, *Who Rules Iran?* p. 50.

sources to proselytizing and organizing supporters abroad, particularly in Lebanon. The IPO, active in Europe, Pakistan, and India, appears to have increased the level of its activities in recent years.

## COMPARING THE SECURITY INSTITUTIONS

In general, the various institutions emphasize different issues, to their mutual satisfaction, though in practice they overlap considerably in their duties. The intelligence services and the IRGC are far more focused on the defense of the revolution from its internal enemies than is the *Artesh*. Often, in their view, this requires attacks on dissidents abroad and coercive actions against Iranian citizens, both of which have implications for Iranian foreign policy. The IRGC also focuses on less traditional defense duties, particularly those that involve unusual missions or capabilities. These duties range from stopping smuggling and controlling Iran's WMD (weapons of mass destruction) and missile forces to preparing for closing the Straits of Hormuz. In contrast, the *Artesh* focuses its efforts on more traditional threats, such as an Iraqi attack.

These different missions affect the institutional ethos of the various security institutions. The *Artesh* is content with a strategy of damage limitation and risk minimization. The IRGC and the Ministry of Intelligence and Security (MOIS), in contrast, are more proactive and interested in actively defending the republic's interests and developing their own niches.[18]

The institutions' respective stars rise and fall according to their match with Iran's overall ambitions. When exporting the revolution or countering internal enemies such as the MKO is deemed vital, the MOIS's and IRGC's profiles rise. When economics, ethnicity, and geopolitics dominate, the *Artesh*'s views become more important.

---

[18]There is little sign that the IRGC's internal security duties are hindering its conduct of broader military operations. Of course, different bits of the IRGC are encouraged to train for different types of operations. The potential danger is that they may not get the appropriate training, etc., with regard to their particular operational activities and parameters.

## THE SECURITY INSTITUTIONS AND IRAN'S MILITARY POSTURE

In general, Iran's limited economic resources and restrictions on its purchases from abroad have prevented military officials from dramatically improving Iran's forces. As Table 4.1 makes clear, Iran has not made a major drive to modernize its forces in the last decade, and most of its force structure is aging. Iran's military budget has stayed relatively limited. Though Iran has made major purchases, including T-72 tanks, MiG-29 fighters, and Kilo submarines, it has not purchased these in large enough numbers to significantly alter the regional military balance.

### Table 4.1

### Selected Iranian Military Order-of-Battle Information

|  | 1989/1990 | 1992 | 1997 |
|---|---|---|---|
| Defense expenditures ($ billion) | 5.77 | 2.3 | 4.7 |
| Total armed forces | 604,500 | 513,000 | 545,600 |
| Main battle tanks (estimates) | Perhaps 500 total: largely T-54/-55; T-62; some T-72; Chieftain Mk3/5; M-47/-48; M-60A1 | Perhaps 1,245 total: including around 150 T-72; 190 T-54/-55; 260 Ch T-59; 150 T-62; 135 M-60A1; 135 M-47/-48 | Some 1,345 total: including 400 T-54/-55 and T-59; 75 T-62; 480 T-72; 140 Chieftain Mk3/5; 150 M-47/-48; 100 M-60A1 |
| Key naval assets | 3 destroyers; 5 frigates; 10 missile craft; 7 amphibious | 2 Kilo submarines; 2 destroyers; 3 frigates; 10 missile craft; 8 amphibious | 3 Kilo submarines; 3 frigates; 9 amphibious; 20 missile craft |
| Key air assets | 4 squadrons F-4D/E; 4 squadrons F-5E/F; 1 squadron with 15 F-14 | 4 squadrons F-4D/E; 4 squadrons F-5E/F; 4 squadrons F-14; 1 squadron F-7; 1 squadron Su-24; 2 squadrons MiG-29 | 4 squadrons F-4D/E; 4 squadrons F-5E/F; 1 squadron Su-24; 2 squadrons MiG-29 |

Source: *The Military Balance* (London, UK: International Institute for Strategic Studies, 1989, 1994, and 1999).

Budget limits aside, Iran's military, however, has influence over several aspects of its own development. These include the drive to build a domestic arms industry, an overall quest for increased military professionalism, an emphasis on missile programs, and a desire to gain WMD. Accomplishing all these goals, however, requires political backing.

## The Drive for Military Autonomy

Iran has made much of the principle of self-sufficiency when arming its conventional forces. In practical terms, this has meant producing arms and spare parts domestically, an enterprise that is both expensive and likely to lead to a larger gap in military technology between Iran and countries armed by the West. Iran's emphasis on self-reliance reflects the lessons it learned from the war with Iraq, when its former Western suppliers refused to sell it arms. As the industry has developed, it has gained its own voice, and it now represents an important domestic interest.

Both the *Artesh* and the IRGC support the domestic arms industry by ordering main battle tanks, howitzers, munitions, and other arms from the state-owned firms affiliated with the logistics wing of the Ministry of Defense. The IRGC is particularly focused on supporting the domestic arms industry and otherwise preserving autonomy. The IRGC usually takes the initiative, but it frequently draws on the *Artesh* to provide expertise.

## A Commitment to Military Professionalism

Iran's commitment to enhanced military professionalism and better military coordination appears secure. Instability along Iran's borders and the formal U.S. military and political presence in the Persian Gulf have increased the premium on Iran's maintaining a modern, well-equipped, and efficient army. Iranian leaders have learned through bitter experience that a ramshackle amateur army of volunteers—an army of "professional martyrs," as some Iranians have called it—is no match against today's armies.[19]  The need, therefore, for a well-equipped and drilled army that can respond in a coordinated fashion to several challenges simultaneously is accepted by almost all of Iran's leaders.

Iran's security policies in the 1990s reflected these concerns.  Iran's rearmament drive of the 1990s required investment in all the services and the import of new military hardware.  More important still, to realize its objectives, the regime had to upgrade its relations with the regular armed forces, giving them due recognition and a greater public presence.  Military parades have again become commonplace, and senior members of Iran's clerical elite seem to make a habit of attending military rallies and of being seen with military officers. Both the IRGC and the *Artesh* have increased their emphasis on professionalism.  They are increasing the technical training offered to soldiers and basing promotion criteria more on education and expertise.

---

[19]Shahram Chubin, *Iran's National Security Policy: Capabilities, Intentions and Impact* (Washington, DC: Carnegie Endowment for International Peace, 1994).

# Chapter Five

# THE MILITARY AND IRANIAN SOCIETY

Iran's military plays an important role in Iranian society. In 1925, leaders from Iran's military deposed the Qajar dynasty, establishing the regime of Reza Shah. Military leaders also played an instrumental role in the 1953 coup against Mosaddeq. (However, the Islamic Republic deliberately tries to guard against this degree of military influence.) Religious leaders (like the Shah before them) try to employ the military to strengthen their positions and ensure their control over Iranian society. Thus, the military's role in security cannot be separated from its overall role in Iran's domestic politics.

This chapter focuses on two issues. It first describes the military's role in Iranian politics today. It then explores the question of whether the armed forces would be loyal to the regime if political strife were to increase.

## THE MILITARY AND THE KHATAMI TRANSFORMATION

The military establishment, both in the IRGC and the *Artesh*, has been re-engaging with Iranian civil society since the 1990s. The *Artesh* is doing this through several channels: providing manpower and technical expertise for civilian projects; playing a leading part in the reconstruction of war-damaged regions of the country; providing more open access to its assets (through military parades, open days, and so on); playing up its diligence to defend Iran against its external enemies (here, Arab and Western anti-Iranian rhetoric has come in handy); and turning its inability to engage in national politics into an advantage by giving the impression of deliberately staying above the factional politics of the regime, presumably for the sake of the nation.

Many among the IRGC and the *Basij* interpret President Khatami's reforms and the ideas of his adherents as challenges to the interests of those who have been loyal supporters of the Islamic Republic and defenders of the *Faqih*. From their perspective, the so-called liberals gathering around Khatami are trying to dismantle their system of privileges and access to power. Conservative political forces often encourage these gloomy perceptions and have encouraged groups such as *Ansar-e Hezballah* and the *Basij* to enter the fray.[1]

In short, the reform process unleashed by President Khatami is now a bone of contention within the defense establishment and its constituent parts in the *Entezamat* (the law and security enforcement agencies) that, without speedy action by the political establishment, could threaten the fabric of the painstakingly created multifaceted defense structure.

Military officers' attitudes toward popular unrest have been decidedly mixed and their overall response inconsistent. There are those among the IRGC who believe that the organization should no longer offer a blind defense of the ruling politico-clerical establishment against domestic pressures or criticism. During the Qazvin riots of 1994, elements within the IRGC refused to carry out orders to enter the city and reestablish order at all costs (including the use of force). In publicized statements and letters after the Qazvin riots, senior serving officers (including those from the IRGC) felt compelled to express their concern to the nation and the regime about the "chaotic economic, cultural, and political situation in the country"—interpreted as direct criticism of the role that clerics have played in national affairs.

However, when these same issues resurfaced in the aftermath of the July 1999 Tehran students riots, the IRGC commanders were concerned with the destabilizing impact of the Khatami administration's political and cultural reforms. Several commanders of the IRGC made public criticism of President Khatami and of his reforms, claiming that the reforms were endangering the *nezam* (revolution-

---

[1]Menashri, "Whither Iranian Politics?" pp. 13-51.

ary order) and that the IRGC could not stand by and see the fruits of the revolution destroyed; it may have no option but to intervene in the interest of the whole Islamic regime.[2]

What followed in this saga suggests the limits of the IRGC's influence.[3] First, the *Artesh* proclaimed that the defense establishment should not have a view on political matters.  Next came the outcry from the President's supporters and the population at large that, under the Islamic Republic, the military has never determined, and would never determine, the fate of the country or issued ultimata against its political leaders.  The authors of the ill-fated letter to the President warning of the dire consequences of his actions and their readiness to act were forced to retract their comments, pledge their commitment to the President, and promise not to express such views again—at least not in public.

These problems are likely to worsen as time goes on, as the more ideologically committed IRGC leaders become distanced from Iranian society.[4]  Today's Iranian youth are proving difficult to sway or control, despite years of Islamization.  Iranian leaders readily admit that today's youth, irrespective of background and upbringing, are not only highly cosmopolitan and culturally diverse, but also open to new ideas and receptive to alien habits.  Indeed, several of Iran's more forward-looking leaders, including President Khatami, have already recognized that the country's limited outlets for social activity and entertainment are driving the youth away from the regime and into the arms of what they call "satanic cultures." Even

---

[2]See *Iran News'* daily coverage of the July 1999 riots for further details.

[3]Saeed Barzin, "Iran: Reining in the Right," *Middle East International*, July 30, 1999, pp. 17-18.

[4]These developments must be seen in the context of a much broader ongoing struggle for the soul of the revolution.  The issue that attracted debate was that of  "moral corruption," which the conservatives had identified as a major social concern and which they had used to great effect as a means of undermining the public policies of the Rafsanjani administration.  The issue of moral corruption, however, was not just a political football.  With around 63 percent of the population under the age of 25, the clerical elite has been genuinely concerned that as a majority of Iranians are now net consumers, not just of goods and services but also of ideas and habits, they could develop a dependence on Western culture, a dependence that the regime has tried hard to eradicate.  For a discussion of these issues, see Anoushiravan Ehteshami, "Iran on the Eve of the New Millennium: Domestic and Regional Perspectives," *FAU Seminar 1997* (Copenhagen, Foreningen Af Udviklingsforskere I Danmark, 1997), pp. 31-47.

worse, the youth seem to readily accept and identify with the "MTV culture," received illegally by many of Iran's average-income urban dwellers.  They also seem to have developed a degree of fondness about the past, fed by the older generation who nostalgically reminisce about how good life was before the revolution.  These trends in turn reinforce the country's secularizing tendency, which the post-1979 security forces abhor.

Yet even as the gap between Iranian society and the politicized elements of the security forces grows, the regime's reliance on coercion may well increase.  Political tensions, infighting, and prolonged economic difficulties have increased the regime's reliance on its coercive machinery.  Social issues may be the most polarizing.  To traditionalist and rightist forces, moreover, the social and cultural realm is the most important dimension that distinguishes Iran from other developing, even Muslim, countries.  In general, however, Iranian elites prefer to avoid direct confrontation and will try other measures to placate opposition.

## ARE THE ARMED FORCES LOYAL?

In general, the armed forces—particularly the IRGC—are a prop for the conservative elements of the regime rather than a threat to them.  Nevertheless, the armed forces' support is lukewarm, particularly when it comes to ensuring the stability of the regime against reformers in Iran itself.[5]

The *Artesh* of today is not likely to become politically active against the Islamic Republic.  The commander of the Armed Forces Joint Staffs, Brigadier General Hassan Firouzabadi, issued a statement in May 1998 criticizing Commander of the IRGC Yahya Rahim Safavi for adopting an overtly political line on domestic issues and for allowing the IRGC to become embroiled in politics.  The Islamic regime, like previous Iranian regimes, has deliberately excluded the military from day-to-day politics.  There would need to be near-total collapse of the government or complete chaos before the *Artesh* would feel bold

---

[5]The military is not likely to play a divisive role if ethnic tension in Iran increases. Although the Iranian military does not trust all ethnicities equally (Kurds, for example, are rare among senior officers), in general the military is open to groups other than Persians.

enough to take matters into its own hands.  Also, the *Artesh* in Iran has always relied on a political master, which it lacks through deliberate design by the revolutionary regime.

There is little chance, also, that the IRGC would rebel against its political masters and decide to find its own solution to Iran's security or political problems.  The IRGC leadership is closely intertwined with the political establishment, and few IRGC officers, if any, would dare to undertake such a risky and dangerous operation without authorization from the Supreme Leader.  Increasingly, however, IRGC leaders see themselves as the vanguard of the revolutionary regime and compare themselves to their counterparts in Turkey and Pakistan, who regularly intervene to ensure that their agendas are respected by politicians.

Most IRGC commanders are on the conservative side of the Iranian political spectrum.  With regard to the defense of the revolutionary system, there is no dispute among the IRGC's leaders.  The dispute, if we can call it that, is over how best to revitalize the system and guarantee its long-term survival—a dispute that currently dominates Iranian politics in general.  Some believe that this can be done only through reform and openness, while others believe that such reforms pose a mortal threat to the character and nature of the Islamic Republic.

The IRGC rank and file, however, appear to reflect the preferences of most Iranians.  A poll conducted by moderate parliament members indicated that 80 percent of IRGC members favored Khatami, while only 9 percent supported more rightist candidates.[6]  Reportedly, 73 percent of the IRGC and 70 percent of the *Basij* voted for Khatami.[7] This is not surprising, as many leading supporters of Khatami are former revolutionaries, having been involved in such defining events as the takeover of the U.S. embassy in Tehran.[8]  Moreover, many of

---

[6]*Gulf States Newsletter*, vol. 24, no. 625, November 24, 1999, p. 6.

[7]Buchta, *Who Rules Iran?* p. 125.

[8]Examples include Ibrahim Asgharzeadeh, Abbas Abdi, and Mohammad Musavi Khoeniha, all of whom are leading reformers.  Many of Khatami's supporters also have distinguished war records.  Others were supporters of former President Hashemi Rafsanjani, such as Ataollah Mohajerani and Gholam-Hossein Karbaschi. See Christo-

the protesters, such as the students who demonstrated in Tehran in July 1999, are the children of IRGC families and other pillars of the revolution.[9]

For the revolutionary leadership, a greater concern is possible IRGC inaction or slow response during a crisis. As noted above, the IRGC leadership reflects the same confusions and complexities that have befallen much of Iran's political elite. If the elite split (particularly if the current supporters of the Supreme Leader are divided), the IRGC's response is not clear. The rank and file are less ideological than their leaders and more sympathetic to calls for reform. While they too would defend the system, they seem interested in the political discourse and more in tune with the people's needs and demands. Again, this does not make them liberals but, rather, more distant from the grand picture. They will, however, obey orders that have to do with defending Iran's borders, defeating the armed opposition, or attacking bandits, gangsters, smugglers, or drug traffickers.

The greatest uncertainty is whether the IRGC would crack down on a widespread, popular reform movement that had the support of many Iranians who claimed to support an Islamic system, albeit a much-reformed one. The IRGC has played a role in suppressing unrest. In July 1995, the IRGC ended an automobile workers' strike in Islamabad.[10] Clearly, many IRGC leaders would be prepared to take action: In response to demonstrations in Tehran in the summer of 1999, 24 IRGC commanders sent a letter to Khatami, which was subsequently leaked to hard-line newspapers, that they would take the law into their own hands unless the President cracked down on the demonstrators.[11] On April 16, 2000, IRGC leaders stated that enemies of the revolution would feel "the reverberating impact of the hammer of the Islamic revolution on their skulls."[12] However,

---

pher de Bellaigue, "The Struggle for Iran," *New York Review of Books*, December 16, 1999, p. 54.

[9]Azar Nifisi, "Student Demonstrations in Iran: What's Next?" *Policywatch*, no. 400, July 21, 1999.

[10]"Protests Near Tehran and in Southwest," Radio Free Europe/Radio Liberty, *Iran Report*, vol. 3, no. 2, January 10, 1999 (electronic version).

[11]A.W. Samii, "The Contemporary Iranian News Media, 1998-1999," *Middle East Review of International Affairs*, vol. 3, no. 4, December 1999 (electronic version).

[12]Radio Free Europe/Radio Liberty, *Iran Report*, vol. 3, no. 17, May 1, 2000.

problems could arise, à la Qazvin in 1994 or Tehran in July 1999, in which the IRGC might be required to quell unrest due to political, economic, and social reasons. Whether they would withdraw their support in another mass urban-based riot or demonstration is hard to predict. Much would depend on the nature of the violence and the position of the political leadership. If the political leadership is divided, so too will be the IRGC's leaders.

To guard against this problem, Iran's leadership appears to have formed special units—so-called *Ashura*, *Zahra*, and *Sayid-ul Shohoda* battalions—to handle the problem of popular unrest. Units of the IRGC and *Basij* have been created to ensure that the regime has trained and available troops that it can call on during a domestic crisis.[13] Interviews suggest that these units number between 10,000 and 12,000, though many are used to guard regime officials or otherwise occupy singular tasks.

## POTENTIAL RED LINES

In Chapters Three and Four, we argue that there is a degree of consensus in Iran that is often obscured by the smoke of everyday politics. Consensus has its limits, however, and greater military intervention in Iran's politics cannot be ruled out.

Potential "red lines" for conflict include the following:

- A threat to the rule of the *Faqih*. The current leadership will tolerate limited reforms, if necessary, as long as the existing order remains secure.

- Open disrespect of Khomeini or for his legacy. All of Iran's elites, both conservatives and reformers, claim to act in the Imam's name. His speeches and acts are used to justify their points of view, even when his legacy is being changed. An open rejection of Khomeini, particularly if it involved open contempt for his legacy, would enrage many stalwarts and might destroy consensus.

---

[13]Radio Free Europe/Radio Liberty, *Iran Report*, vol. 2, no. 36, September 13, 1999, and Buchta, *Who Rules Iran?* pp. 66 and 125.

- Social reforms that threaten the existing view or equilibrium of society. Marginal changes to improve the status of women or religious minorities can be tolerated, but dramatic reforms may provoke a traditionalist backlash.

- Jeopardizing the unity or sanctity of the state. Iranian elites of all political stripes share a basic Islamo-Persian nationalism that rejects territorial claims by neighboring states or calls for greater autonomy by ethnic minorities. Measures that might threaten existing borders or sovereignty would be resisted.

- Moving too close to Israel or the United States. One particular stream of the Imam's legacy is rejection of ties to Israel or Washington. Openly flouting this would anger important segments of the security establishment.

In general, consensus is easier to achieve in the area of security policy than in the area of economic and social policies, where far more interests are involved and the issues touch cornerstones of the revolution more directly.

Despite the existence of these red lines, the military institutions are likely to be forces for stability. If politics remain stable and avoid widespread strife, the IRGC leadership would prefer to devote its attention to improving its military standards and competing more effectively with the *Artesh*. Intervention is more likely if internal divisions deepen at the elite level, ideological fault lines widen, and factionalism turns violent. If the current factionalist politics were to escalate to the point of widespread violence, not only might elements from the IRGC become embroiled, but serious challenges might be posed for the national security forces, whose job it is to keep order. If armed gangs were to be deployed by various power centers, the *Artesh* would find it almost impossible to escape involvement, particularly if the (largely externally based) opposition groups were to capitalize on the regime's infighting to wage a protracted campaign of terror against its leading elements. However, this alarmist scenario must be tempered by the IRGC's own recognition of its internal divisions. The IRGC would risk a further marginalization of its position if it aggressively and directly opposed further moderation in Iran's domestic politics.

# Chapter Six

# IMPACT ON FOREIGN POLICY

Iran's foreign policy is too complex for simple description and prediction. However, the fundamental sources and security institutions described earlier shape both its direction and its application. The direction of Iran's foreign policy is hardly consistent: At times, the revolutionary imperative dominates; at other times, concerns over ethnic fragmentation or economic relations predominate. Nevertheless, patterns do emerge that can be described in some detail.

The armed forces and intelligence services will play an essential role in many of these decisions, particularly with regard to how Iran can best meet its security challenges. Although these institutions often play, at most, a limited role in formulating Iran's objectives, their decisions shape the means used to pursue these ends.

This chapter first notes the issues over which the security institutions have the most influence. It then describes the factors that shape Iran's relations with its neighbors, key regional countries, and the United States. It concludes by assessing factors that shape Iran's decisionmaking for other vital security concerns, such as support for insurgents abroad and Iran's military posture.

For these various objectives, this chapter notes both Iran's overall behavior and the specific agendas of its security institutions. The discussion emphasizes the perspectives of the IRGC and the *Artesh*, though other institutions and organizations are also often important.

## WHERE THE SECURITY INSTITUTIONS MATTER MOST

The *Artesh* has a wide remit in terms of assessing and advising on national security issues, so in this sense its influence is far more functional and institutional than geographic. The *Artesh*'s influence is most directly felt in weapons acquisition, training and military exercises, and the annual round of budget negotiations. It cannot, however, choose its military suppliers and is guided in this regard by Tehran's political calculations and budgetary constraints.

The IRGC, largely due to its revolutionary origins and ties to the Supreme Leader's office, is influential in the broad area of Islamic revolution abroad. According to the IRGC's commander, Yahya Rahim Safavi, "The IRGC has no geographical border. The Islamic revolution is the border of the IRGC."[1] It has an extensive network of contacts across the Muslim world, with a particular emphasis on Lebanon, Iraq, the Gulf region, and the wider Arab world in general. Thus, geographically speaking, the IRGC's realm is the Middle East and North Africa, including the two Muslim countries to Iran's east, Afghanistan and Pakistan. The IRGC is far weaker with regard to Europe and to the West in general.

The IRGC's influence over foreign affairs is declining. It is good at being reactive, and sometimes even good at being proactive, but it is less of a player in the patient game of statecraft, foreign policy building, and conducting Iran's external affairs. The regime's confidence in the IRGC to conduct a long war has declined.[2]

In general, hard-and-fast rules as to which institutions govern which policy offer little insight. The large number of actors important to Iranian decisionmaking and the conflicting forces that push Iran in different ways lead to policies that often vary by country, by issue, and by the issues of the day in Tehran. Key individuals often change institutions, and their responsibilities and networks go with them. Perhaps most important, different regime priorities lead to the rise and fall of different institutional agendas.

---

[1] *Salam*, June 3, 1998.

[2] Buchta, *Who Rules Iran?* p. 147.

## RELATIONS WITH REGIONAL STATES AND OTHER IMPORTANT POWERS

As the discussion above indicates, Iran's foreign policy varies considerably. The factors noted in Chapter Two—Islam, nationalism, geopolitics, ethnicity, and economics—all play roles in shaping policy. So too do the particular agendas and concerns of Iran's security institutions. Thus, to gain a full understanding of Iran's security policy, it is necessary to assess Iran's behavior on a country-by-country basis.

### Iraq

Although Iraq remains Iran's gravest security concern and most bitter foe, Tehran is cautious with regard to encouraging unrest in Iraq. Iran favors the containment of Iraq in general, but it opposes any action that might fragment its neighbor.

Both in and out of Iran's security establishment, Iraq is viewed as the greatest threat to Iran's security.[3] The eight-year war with Iraq haunts Iran today. Iraq remains hostile, and discoveries about its extensive WMD programs have alarmed Tehran. Iraq's regime is viewed as highly revisionist, with designs on controlling the Shatt al-Arab and Arab-populated parts of Iran. The immediacy of concerns has abated somewhat in the last decade, however, as the U.S.-led containment of Iraq has sapped Baghdad's military and economic strength. Nevertheless, Iraq is Iran's leading short-term as well as long-term security threat.

Both Iran and Iraq also harbor each other's political opponents. Iran supports a Shi'a opposition force in Iraq (the Supreme Council of the Islamic Revolution in Iraq, or SCIRI) to gain leverage over Baghdad. Iraq does the same with Iran by supporting the *Mujahedin-e Khalq* Organization (MKO), a Marxist and nominally Islamist movement. Policies toward these groups can be seen as barometers of relations: Assassinations and unrest are actively encouraged when relations between the two countries are poor, and the groups are reined in when relations are improving.

---

[3]Private discussions with Iranian officials.

Iran also seeks to exploit Kurdish hostility toward Baghdad while preventing that hostility from becoming a strong force that could spill over into Iran itself. This tactic began well before the Islamic revolution, when Iran used Iraq's Kurdish opposition under Mustafa Barzani to pressure Iraq, dropping support for the Kurds in 1975 after Iraq agreed to Iran's terms on their disputed border. Today, Iran encourages the reconciliation of the Mas'ud Barzani–led Kurdish Democratic Party (KDP) with the Talibani-led Patriotic Union of Kurdistan (PUK) in the hopes of keeping the forces viable as a major irritant to Saddam's regime.[4]

Iran's policy toward Iraq and the Kurds is indicative of its concern for regional stability. Despite Iran's hostility toward Saddam's government and repeated backing of the Kurds, Iran opposes any arrangement that might embolden the Iraqi Kurds to set up their own government or state. Iran has supported measures to reconcile the various Kurdish factions in Iraq.[5]

Concerns over restive minorities and regional instability have even led Iran to limit its support for Iraqi Shi'as in recent years—a dramatic change from the early days of the revolution, when Ayatollah Khomeini and other regime leaders called on Iraqi Shi'as to revolt. Iran has not extended large-scale support for the Shi'as in Iraq, even when Baghdad engaged in massive repression, as in 1991. Baghdad's violence against the Shi'a leadership evokes criticisms, and Iraqi Shi'as are permitted to demonstrate in Tehran, but more concrete

---

[4]James Blitz, "D'Alema Seeks Positive Solution to Ocalan Dilemma," *Financial Times,* November 18, 1998.

[5]On the fighting between the Kurds and the Turkish government, former president Hashemi Rafsanjani's comments are indicative: "The fighting in northern Iraq gives Iran a headache and causes many problems. Large groups that flee the fighting are taking refuge in Iran, bringing scores of problems with them. These groups smuggle weapons into Iran. The animals they bring with them sometimes cause epidemics. Naturally, in order to avoid such problems we want peace to reign in Iraq. We expect Turkey to understand our problems." *Canal-7* (Istanbul, in Turkish), June 16, 1997, BBC ME/2949 MED/11-12, June 19, 1997. See also Alan Phillips, "Iranians Watch and Wait as Shi'ite Cousins Suffer," *Sunday Telegraph,* February 28, 1999, p. 21, and Saideh Lotfian, "Iran's Middle East Policies Under President Khatami," *The Iranian Journal of International Affairs,* vol. X, no. 4, Winter 1998-1999, p. 431.

measures are lacking.[6]  Iran has initiated a limited dialog with Iraq that is intended to facilitate pilgrimages by Iranian Shi'as to holy places in Iraq.

A minority view in Iran calls for a reconciliation with Iraq.  Some leaders argue that it is in Iran's long-term interest to improve Iran-Iraq relations, particularly while Baghdad remains vulnerable and under international sanctions.  Such a relationship, they argue, would give Iran a bigger say in Iraq's future, provide it with leverage over the current regime, and weaken the U.S. presence in the area. But the proponents of the pro-Iraq policy are still a small minority in Iran.  Most Iranians, including large segments of the IRGC and the *Basij*, abhor President Saddam Hussein's regime and feel that they owe it to the martyrs of the war to help bring about the regime's end. Indeed, the martyrs factor is the most effective barrier against a new opening toward Iraq, despite Baghdad's repeated offers.

Despite the emotion and bitterness that characterize Iranians' sentiments toward the Baath regime, Tehran is willing to act pragmatically to advance its interests.  Iran and Iraq have fitful diplomatic contact.  Tehran has, for a price, helped Iraq smuggle oil and otherwise evade international restrictions, even as Iran's leaders have kept a wary eye on Iraq's military and WMD capabilities.

Iraq's position in the Iranian consciousness is also unique for historical and religious reasons.  Iraq is, in essence, a second Shi'a homeland.  Two of the great pilgrimage shrines and centers of Shi'a religious learning—the cities of Najaf and Karbala—are in Iraq, as are many lesser but important places of veneration.  Many Iranian religious leaders studied in Iraq, and contacts between the communities, though cut significantly since Saddam Hussein consolidated power, have historically been strong.

## Agendas of Iran's Security Institutions

Iraq remains at the center of Iran's security concerns for both the *Artesh* and the IRGC.  In general, the *Artesh* focuses on the conven-

---

[6]For an example of Iran's weak reaction after the assassination of Muhammid Sadiq Sadr and his two sons in Najaf in February 1999, see *IRNA*, February 23, 1999, BBC ME/3648 MED/8, February 25, 1999.

tional threat Iraq poses, relying on defensive measures to ensure that Iran is prepared to face a resurgent Iraq. The IRGC is more focused on anti-MKO operations and on working with the Iraqi Shi'as, both of which demand offensive measures. In practice, however, the duties of the *Artesh* and the IRGC overlap considerably.

The *Artesh* remains fearful of the Iraqi regime's posturing toward Iran and has contingency plans for renewed Iraqi provocations over the Shatt al-Arab border issue. Although the *Artesh* calculates that Iraq's remaining SSM (surface-to surface missile) force does not give it the capability to strike at Tehran, the *Artesh* does not rule out the possible deployment of SSMs against Iran's urban and industrial centers nearer the border.[7]

An associated concern is the resurgence of Iraq's WMD capability, which *Artesh* leaders think can be restored in the absence of international inspectors. To deter Iraq, Iran has been developing its own counterforce, which includes a large SSM capability and the deployment of Russian-supplied long-range strike aircraft. It has also been building up its air defense systems around strategic targets.

The cross-border military operations of the MKO are a cause of concern for the *Artesh* and the IRGC alike. Iranian armed forces regularly attack MKO facilities (with aircraft and missiles) deep inside Iraq, a pattern that, in the absence of a formal peace treaty between Tehran and Baghdad, is likely to continue.

The IRGC sees itself as a defender of the Iraqi Shi'as. The IRGC is heavily engaged in training and maintaining the military wing of Iraqi Islamic insurgent groups such as the SCIRI and Al-Da'wa. The Ministry of Intelligence and Security (MOIS) assists it in these activities. The IRGC has prepared itself for swift action should Baghdad become more vulnerable in the south, or should its worsening situation require greater Iranian intervention. The IRGC's Iraqi Shi'a allies are actively engaged in anti-MKO operations, penetrating Iraqi territory.

---

[7]*Iran News*, February 6, 1998. Key targets will include Iran's nuclear infrastructure and its oil industry, both within easy reach of Iraqi aircraft and SSMs.

In contrast to its situation in many other policy areas, the defense establishment has considerable influence over Iran's policy toward Iraq. Tehran develops its Iraq strategy through the intelligence, and clandestine operations that the IRGC, military intelligence, and the MOIS conduct in Iraq, and through the information that the Iran-based Shi'a opposition groups bring. Thus, despite the recommendation of several radical elements in Tehran that Iran should throw its lot in with Iraq and form an anti-U.S. front with Syria and Iraq, the military institutions' threat assessment of Iraq and their calculations about the negative impact on Iran's national security of such an alliance continue to hold sway. The *Artesh* regards any alliance with Iraq as pure adventurism, a term also used by President Khatami himself.

## Russia

Russia's relations with Iran have become friendly, if hardly close, despite Russia's history of imperialism and past attempts to annex Iranian territories. Moreover, relations have improved despite Moscow's brutal war against Muslims in Afghanistan and two wars against Muslim Chechens.

The explanation for this closeness is pragmatic necessity. Iran's cultivation of the Soviet Union and then Russia started during the war with Iraq. Soviet-manufactured arms took the place of U.S. and other embargoed Western arms. This created a link, especially with regard to aircraft, which Iran has sought to tighten.[8] Nuclear technology embargoed by the United States and its allies was also supplied by Russia, which professes to see no proliferation threat from Iran. Thus, Russia, while certainly not the supplier of choice, has become the supplier of necessity.

The relationship is businesslike rather than based on shared interests or warm intergovernment relations. The technology transfers and training that Moscow supplies remain strictly tied to Iran's capacity

---

[8]The first supplies of Soviet-type equipment came from North Korea and China, followed by direct arms agreements with Moscow. A similar pattern emerged with Scud missiles. Iran first received Scud missiles and technology from Syria and Libya. Later, North Korea and China filled the gap, after which Iran received technology transfers from Russia.

to pay. This was evident in the transfer of the three Kilo-class submarines, whose delivery was staggered accordingly. This feeling is mutual and suggests that Tehran does not have any illusions that it has gained in terms of reliability or sophistication in exchanging the United States for Russia as a supplier of technology.

Since the fall of the Soviet Union, Iran also has cultivated Russia to offset U.S. dominance. Iran, like Russia, China, and India, sees the emergence of a unipolar world as troubling enough to encourage at least thinking about offsetting geopolitical axes. This effort, however, has produced little actual cooperation, and Moscow remains suspicious of Iran's regional ambitions and support for Muslim movements.

As it has in general regarding restive minorities, Iran has tried to foster stability rather than encourage unrest in areas of mutual interest to Russia. Iran first signaled this preference in 1989 when it sought, unsuccessfully, to use its influence in the Muslim parts of the Soviet Union to discourage unrest that might contribute to the breakup of the state. Since then, Iran has avoided excessive criticism of Russian repression of the Muslim parts of the former Soviet Union. In exchange for technology and stability, the Islamic Republic has been willing to swallow its principles and abandon Muslim solidarity.

Chechnya illustrates Iran's hard-nosed realpolitik policy toward Russia. Although making polite noises about human rights, Iran has avoided harsh and open condemnation of Russia, despite the deaths of thousands of Muslim civilians. Iranian leaders have consistently referred to Chechnya as an "internal matter."[9]

Iran's and Russia's interests may overlap in regard to wanting regional stability, opposing U.S. hegemony, and conducting a mutually beneficial arms trade, but the two are more likely to be rivals on other fronts. A resurgent Russia with a revived nationalism is not likely to be an easy or desirable neighbor. The Caucasus and Central Asia remain potential areas of conflict. Iran and Russia both seek to prevent U.S. influence in the Caucasus from growing but are far from agreeing on their respective roles. It is not in Iran's interest that

---

[9]Radio Free Europe/Radio Liberty, *Iran Report*, vol. 2, no. 45, December 15, 1999 (electronic version).

Russia dominate the former southern Soviet republics. Nor do Iran and Russia share economic or energy interests. Iran would like to be the principal energy route for exports from the region, whether via the Persian Gulf or across Iran to South Asia. So too would Russia.

## Agendas of Iran's Security Institutions

The concerns of the *Artesh* are important factors in shaping Iran's policy toward Russia, while those of the IRGC—which are far more ambivalent—play less of a role.

The *Artesh* views Moscow as a possible, though hardly dependable, ally against U.S. pressure and as an important source of military hardware and software. Some officers, while complaining about the Russian suppression of the Chechen rebels, speak positively of Russia's role in helping the Iranian armed forces and stabilizing Central Asia, particularly with regard to countering the Taliban's influence. The *Artesh* looks to Russia for training and also for the supply of spares and technical know-how. The *Artesh* hopes to gain from the transfer of Russian satellite and space technologies and of Russian airframe materials, technologies, and avionics. The *Artesh* also hopes that improved political relations with Russia and India will mean that it can pursue tripartite military exchanges and exploit India's vast experience in Soviet military hardware and technologies for its own military R&D purposes.[10]

The IRGC is far more critical of Russia, but it swallows its concerns for realpolitik reasons. The IRGC is a close observer of Russia's brutal strategy in the Caucasus and is more critical of its military operations in Chechnya. There have even been unconfirmed reports that the IRGC had intended to send volunteers and to provide training for Chechen fighters. It sees Russia as a decadent, weak, and corrupt society, which colors its perspective on Iranian-Russian relations. The IRGC's concern, however, is tempered by its reliance on Russia for many weapons systems and support technology.

---

[10]Iran has also been pursuing a parallel tripartite military tie-up based on a partnership among itself, China, and India.

The focus of Iran's intelligence agencies is on locating Russian military secrets and identifying key Russian personnel who can help Iran's military and other industries.

## China

In the past decade, China has had more-extensive military relations with Iran than with any other country except Pakistan and possibly North Korea. Beijing has sold to Iran thousands of tanks, artillery pieces, and armored personnel carriers; more than 100 fighters; and dozens of small warships. Beijing has also sold to Iran an array of missile systems and technology, including air-to-air missiles, surface-to-air missiles, and anti-shipping cruise missiles. Most worrisome has been China's transfer of ballistic missile technology and its assistance with Iran's WMD programs. China's transfers include a range of items that helped Iran build its WMD infrastructure, improve the expertise of its scientists and technicians, and otherwise develop its WMD capabilities. Cooperation in these areas continued at a robust pace until at least October 1997, when China, in part due to U.S. pressure, agreed to suspend or curtail transfers of WMD-related items and anti-shipping missile systems and technology[11] and to provide no new assistance to Iran's nuclear programs. In January 1998, U.S. Secretary of Defense William Cohen received an assurance from Chinese President Jiang Xemin that China would not transfer additional anti-shipping cruise missiles or technology to Iran or help it with indigenous production.[12]

The commercial benefits of China's sales to Iran have been considerable, particularly during the Iran-Iraq war. China sold billions of dollars to the Islamic Republic during the 1980s, and these sales provided Beijing with much-needed foreign currency and an important source of exports. Since the end of the Iran-Iraq war, the volume of Beijing's sales to Iran has fallen considerably—while China's overall trade has skyrocketed—but export earnings are still an important

---

[11]For a complete review of China's arms transfers, see Daniel L. Byman and Roger Cliff, *China's Arms Sales: Motivations and Implications* (Santa Monica, CA: RAND, 1999).

[12]Shirley A. Kan, *Chinese Proliferation of Weapons of Mass Destruction: Current Policy Issues* (Washington, DC: Congressional Research Service Brief, March 23, 1998), p. 6.

source of income for some of China's cash-strapped defense industries.

China's arms sales to Iran are made for foreign policy reasons and for commercial reasons, however. Until recently, China had a strong strategic and political interest in close ties to Iran, as China's leaders considered Iran a bulwark against Soviet expansion in the region. Even today, Beijing appreciates Tehran's attempts to avoid aligning closely with Russia or the United States.[13] And because most regional oil-producing states are close allies of the United States, Beijing seeks to ensure at least a modicum of influence in the region by maintaining good relations with Tehran.

Beijing also recognizes that preventing Iran from improving its military is a U.S. priority, and it may exploit U.S. sensitivity on this issue to attempt to influence U.S. policies in other areas. For example, after the United States announced it was selling F-16s to Taiwan, China revived a proposed transfer of M-11 missiles to Iran that had earlier been canceled due to U.S. pressure.[14] Ties to Iran thus provide Beijing with additional leverage in negotiations with the United States.

Chinese interest in maintaining the flow of oil has so far led Beijing to cultivate relations with Tehran, though this could change in the coming years. China's dependence on imported oil has grown steadily since 1994, and it is likely to do so in the future. Thus, China seeks allies in key oil-producing regions, such as the Persian Gulf. In a crisis, these countries would not likely sell China oil on preferential terms, but Chinese analysts believe that maintaining good relations with leading oil-exporting nations such as Iran is important to China's future energy security.[15] The United States, however, has attempted to convince Beijing that Iranian-backed instability threatens to interrupt the free flow of oil from the Gulf, which could drive up the price of oil and jeopardize China's economic growth. U.S. officials claimed that China's promises to cut nuclear cooperation

---

[13]Bates Gill, *Silkworms and Summitry: Chinese Arms Exports to Iran* (New York: The Asia and Pacific Rim Institute of the American Jewish Committee, 1997), p. 7.

[14]Gill, *Silkworms and Summitry*, p. 21.

[15]Interviews conducted with Chinese security analysts of the Institute of West Asian and African Studies, Chinese Academy of Social Sciences, June 1998.

with Iran made at the October 1997 summit occurred in large part because China recognized this danger.[16]

Iran, for its part, sees China as an important political partner and as a source of weapons systems. China, with its UN seat and resistance to U.S. hegemony, was one of the few major powers willing to maintain strong and cordial relations with Tehran even during the more heady days of the revolutionary regime. Perhaps more important, Tehran greatly appreciated Beijing's willingness to support Iran's missile and nuclear, biological, and chemical (NBC) programs. Moreover, since Iran, like China, seeks to avoid import dependence, Beijing is often a preferred partner because it has been willing to transfer knowledge, expertise, and critical subsystems as well. This has enabled Iran to produce its own variants of Chinese cruise and ballistic missile systems.

In recent years, China's relations with Iran appear to have cooled, and the transfer of arms has fallen in turn. The ending of the Iran-Iraq war and the low price of oil mean that Iran no longer has the need or the ability to buy large quantities of Chinese arms. U.S. sanctions and Iran's economic mismanagement have caused grave economic problems for the Islamic Republic, forcing it to reduce its defense budget. For its part, China no longer sees Iran as a vital bulwark against Russian expansion. Indeed, China often cooperates with Russia against the West. U.S. pressure and China's desire to be seen as a responsible power make Iran a potentially costly friend. U.S. pressure played a major role in Beijing's October 1997 decision to curtail military cooperation with Iran.

### *Agendas of Iran's Security Institutions*

Iran's security institutions appear to share the broader regime's goals of cultivating China as a way of balancing the United States. In addition, they recognize that China can act as an important arms supplier, particularly for missiles and nonconventional systems.

---

[16]"A New China Embracing Nuclear Nonproliferation," *International Herald Tribune*, December 11, 1997, p. 1.

China, however, is not Iran's preferred partner for most conventional systems. The U.S. success in Desert Storm had highlighted to Tehran the importance of advanced weaponry. After the Persian Gulf war, Tehran bought advanced submarines, fighter aircraft, tanks, and surface-to-air missiles from Russia: The Chinese systems, while cheaper, were clearly inferior. Only after 1995, when Russia pledged that it would not make further arms contracts with Iran, did Tehran resume looking to China for conventional arms. In addition, Iranian military officials have shown little faith in the quality of Chinese weapons: During the Iran-Iraq war, they sought to avoid using Chinese systems whenever possible during important battles.

## Turkey

During much of the Cold War, Tehran and Ankara cooperated with the West and with each other against the Soviet Union. Each state felt that Moscow was expansionist—both had faced possible Russian occupation of parts of their territories in the immediate aftermath of World War Two—and decided to swap neutrality for the safer posture of alignment with the West. As non-Arab states that had not been colonized, Iran and Turkey found that they often shared perspectives on the world's problems.

Since the revolution, Iran has had an uneasy relationship with Turkey. Ankara found Iran's support for Turkey's Islamist elements in the 1980s and 1990s provocative. Iran, for its part, avoided close relations due to Turkey's ties to the West and avowed secularism. Nevertheless, their mutual anti-Soviet sentiment and the legacy of previous cooperation contributed to polite relations. However, the potential for volatile relations remains high given the two countries' strategic competition and differing world views.

In general, Iran and Turkey share goals with regard to Iraq. Both oppose Saddam Hussein's regime. Moreover, both balance this hostility with a concern for massive instability in Iraq. In the wake of the war, together with Syria, they consulted to ensure a coordinated approach in the event Iraq was to fragment. Iran has opposed Turkey's periodic incursions into Iraq in search of Kurdish Workers' Party (PKK) elements that have sought sanctuary there. Yet this opposition appears token at most. Both countries fear a strong Iraqi Kurdish movement that might embolden minorities in their own countries.

(Of course, Iran's anti-Kurdish policies at home have not led it to cut its ties to the PKK, which Iran sees as necessary for leverage with Ankara.)

The prediction that Iran and Turkey would inevitably compete for influence in the Caucasus and Central Asia has not come to pass. Iran, however well situated geographically, lacks capital and is regarded by the governments in the region with caution and skepticism. The U.S.-led embargo has also handicapped Iran's diplomacy in the region. Accordingly, Iran has trimmed down whatever ambitions it may have had to ensuring its national interests and emphasizing its cultural and historical connections, rather than the Islamic element, with the Caucasian and Central Asian states. Turkey, by contrast, has benefited from U.S. support, generally and with regard to the construction of a pipeline to bring Caspian oil to the market. Turkey, however, is handicapped by geography in that it has little direct access to the Caucasus–Central Asia region, and the region provides few immediate economic prospects. If anything, Iran and Turkey share common interests in containing conflicts and limiting Russian influence. As a result of this combination of mutual interests and prudence, rivalry between Iran and Turkey is low-key and restrained.

Turkey's membership in NATO and its cooperation with Israel raise the most difficulties for Iran. In recent years, both the *Artesh* and the IRGC have worried about the burgeoning Israeli-Turkish alliance and the access to Iran's borders that this alliance might offer Israel. Iran's leaders have expressed their fears to Ankara, drawn closer to Syria, and broadened their regional contacts by working more closely with rivals of Turkey, such as Greece, Armenia, and Georgia. Of more concern to Turkey, Iran recently increased support for the PKK—support that led to a direct, if very small, clash between the two militaries in July 1999.[17]

---

[17]Iran claims that Turkish troops in July 1999 attacked sites in Iran as part of their anti-PKK campaign. Turkey claims that these were sites in northern Iraq and questions the presence of Iranians there. A joint commission to discuss security was revitalized, and a parliamentary friendship group was created. Iran assured Turkey that its eastern border would remain safe and secure. See the comments of Hojjat el Eslam Hasan Rowhani, Vice-Speaker of the Majles, *IRNA* (in English), BBC ME/3700 MED/7, November 24, 1999. See also the brief report on the incident in *Le Monde*, July 20, 1999, p. 7.

Tehran's residual support for Islam abroad causes problems for Turkey as well. Turkish Prime Minister Bulent Ecevit has accused Iran of seeking to export its ideology to Turkey. As long as Iran perceives Turkey's cooperation with Israel as aimed at itself, its support for the PKK, and perhaps Turkish Islamist groups, will continue.

Despite these irritants, the prognosis for better relations—or for at least no major downturn—remains positive. Iran and Turkey have no disputed borders, no notable historical resentments, and no other sources of disagreement. Both share common, or at least not conflicting, goals in Central Asia and in Iraq. Moreover, there is considerable scope for economic cooperation between the two states. Iran has oil and gas that it can export to energy-thirsty Turkey, and Iran can act as a transit route of energy exports from Turkmenistan and Kazakhstan. Close cooperation, however, awaits the resolution of Iran's problems with the United States, which has strongly protested Ankara's cooperation with Tehran.

## Agendas of Iran's Security Institutions

The *Artesh* views Turkey as a powerful neighbor with a large military machine, strong security and military ties with the West, and a substantial presence on Iran's western (in northern Iraq) and northern (in Azerbaijan and Turkmenistan) borders. Despite Turkey's politico-military superiority, in recent years Iranian leaders have taken a series of potshots at its secular leadership, which has annoyed Ankara and forced it to respond in kind. This has also increased the pressure on the *Artesh* to plan for a possible escalation in political hostilities. In response, the *Artesh* has strengthened its military facilities in Iranian Azerbaijan and has reinforced several of its border posts on the Iran-Turkey border.

The tense border military exchanges between Iran and Turkey and Turkey's free hand in Iraqi Kurdistan have increased the *Artesh*'s fears of instability in Iranian Kurdish regions. In addition, some officers voice the opinion that Turkey's Pan-Turanists are looking for a land corridor through Iran to Azerbaijan and that Iran should put in place a defense plan along its western territories. But a Pan-Turkic onslaught is not seen as a serious threat to Iran. The *Artesh* is more worried about the security impact of Azeri-Turkish relations in the context of Baku's anti-Persian propaganda and its campaign to divorce Iranian Azerbaijan from Iranian territory.

The *Artesh* is particularly worried about the growing relationship between Turkey and Israel. *Artesh* leaders see this partnership as posing a possible direct threat to the country's security and exposing Iran's vital western and central territories (the country's most important regions economically and demographically) to the Israeli armed forces and intelligence-gathering services. It is believed in Tehran that the Turkish-Israeli partnership gives Israel the opportunity to spy on the Iranian border and enables the two countries to train Iran's Kurds while also enabling Turkey to suppress the PKK in eastern Turkey. Tehran also believes that Turkish intelligence has given the Mossad access to information about Iran and about Iranian residents in and visitors to Turkey.

The *Artesh* does not want a military confrontation with a NATO member and close ally of the United States. Some *Artesh* strategists are also concerned that a confrontation with Turkey will adversely affect Iran's relations with the European Union, Iran's main trading partner and a possible future source of military hardware and expertise.

The military tensions with Turkey in the summer of 1999 suggest the *Artesh*'s caution. Clearly, the *Artesh* was suffering from wounded pride when Turkish forces struck at Iranian-backed PKK elements— hence the air force's maneuvers on the Iran-Turkey border in mid-August. Tehran, however, returned the two captured Turkish soldiers and chose not to escalate the situation by retaliating against the Turkish military's provocation. This incident raised the *Artesh*'s threat assessment of Turkey and its level of preparedness in western Iran. However, the *Artesh* advised caution in the internal debate about the border incursion, arguing that after a show of force the situation should be contained.

The IRGC is engaged in the Turkish debate for domestic security reasons. The core reason is the Israeli connection: The IRGC sees its role as conducting counterintelligence activities vis-à-vis the Israelis in Turkey on the one hand, and pressing Turkey to limit its relationship with Israel on the other. The latter, Turkish sources allege, is being done through increased Iranian (IRGC and MOIS) support for the Kurdish separatists and development of links with Turkey's burgeoning Islamist movement.

The IRGC is also concerned by Turkey's secularism and close ties to the West. Ankara embodies a direct challenge to the ideals of the Islamic revolution, and its economic success and foreign policy influence challenge the model offered by Iran.

The MOIS's interest in Turkey stems from Turkey's contacts with the West. The MOIS also monitors the presence of a large Iranian community living and working in the country whose members can enter Turkey without a visa and often transit Turkey to and from Syria.

## Afghanistan

Afghanistan is a difficult and dangerous issue for Iran's rulers. The flow of drugs, the problem of kidnapping, and the threat of Islamic instability emanating from Afghanistan are viewed as major threats in Iran. There is agreement that, perhaps next to Iraq, the Taliban pose the most serious threat to Iran's security today—but the nature of that threat is amorphous.[18] Like Iraq, Iran feels a certain affinity and responsibility for the Shi'a population located in the Hazarajat province. And, also like Iraq, Iran has found itself unable to act effectively as that Shi'a population's protector. Iran hosts around 2 million Afghan refugees, many of whom have resided in Iran for over 20 years. Afghanistan is also a major source of illegal drugs that enter Iran. Finally, the Taliban have provided a haven and support to the MKO and to Sunni radicals who oppose the regime in Tehran. Unlike with Iraq, however, the Taliban do not pose a threat to Iran's territorial integrity, and their military forces are weak. Iran's leaders believe they can contain the Taliban by fostering their own loyal proxies among Afghanistani Shi'a and by working with the Taliban's other enemies.

Tehran is particularly alarmed by the Taliban's consolidation of power in Afghanistan. The Taliban are virulently anti-Shi'a and have cracked down brutally on the Shi'as of the Hazarajat. Moreover, the Taliban are primarily Pashtun and have subjugated Persian-speaking

---

[18]Private discussions with Iranian officials.

Tajiks.   The Taliban's leadership is hostile to Iran, seeing it (quite rightly) as a supporter of its Shi'a foes and of its opponents in general.

A direct conflict almost occurred after the Taliban overran Mazar-e Sharif in mid-1998.  In attacking and then massacring large numbers of Shi'as, including a number of Iranian diplomats, the Taliban challenged Tehran directly.  Iran mobilized its forces and reinforced its frontier, warning of serious consequences.  But Iran was unwilling to get involved in the Afghan civil war.  Iran could only repeat the need for a solution that transcended ethnic divisions.

Tehran has abandoned its revolutionary goal of creating a pro-Iranian Islamic state.  Iran's preferred outcome is to preserve something close to the status quo:[19] no redrawing of the map or reconfiguration of the power balance between state and minorities. The risk of fragmentation in Afghanistan has underscored Iran's stake in regional order.  Iran has in recent years sought to promote a formula for peace in Afghanistan that includes all major ethnic groups in a national coalition.[20]

---

[19]As former president Rafsanjani observed: "Because of the multiethnic nature of Afghanistan, the issue cannot be settled by force, or by the supremacy of one group. That is a recipe for continued conflict."  He went on to say:  "We are against the Talibans or Afghans or seminarians.  We are opposed to their belligerent ideas, warmongering, and their unprincipled acts.  For us there is no differences [sic] between Tajiks and Pashtuns."  Hashemi Rafsanjani, *Vision of IRI, Network 1* (Tehran), BBC ME/3304 MED/1-5, August 15, 1998.  Supreme Leader Ayatollah Khamene'i took the same line: "Of course there was discord, tribal strife.  However, it was not serious and was not coupled with the use of religious, tribal, and nationality prejudices. Unfortunately, it is like this now."  *Voice of IRI* (Tehran), September 15, 1998, BBC ME/3334 MED, September 17, 1998.  An Iranian radio commentary aired the prevailing Iranian view:  "The fact must be accepted that the Afghan community is a multiethnic, and although it is possible for one group to extend its dominance over the whole of Afghanistan through military power, it will not mean the ending of the crisis." *Voice of IRI*, August 9, 1998, BBC ME/3302 MED/21, August 11, 1998.

[20]Tehran may be shifting its policy and recognizing the Taliban's dominant position. As the Taliban have extended their power, Iran has moved to recognize the inevitable and to deal pragmatically with it.  See Pamela Constable, "Afghan Town Praises Iran as Nearby Border Opens to Trade," *International Herald Tribune*, December 23, 1999, p. 1.

## Agendas of Iran's Security Institutions

For the *Artesh*, instability in Afghanistan and adventurism by the Taliban pose a potential threat. The *Artesh* also worries that further suppression of the Shi'a minority in Afghanistan might force Iran to take more direct action in their defense and get the military embroiled in an open-ended conflict in Afghanistan. The *Artesh*'s agenda, therefore, is to contain the Taliban threat and deter it by show of force.[21] *Artesh* leaders do not, however, believe that there exists a military solution to the Afghan problem.

The *Artesh*'s views are shared among Iran's political leadership. Despite the urging of the IRGC, the *Artesh* did not support an attack on Afghanistan after the Mazar-e Sharif slaughter, because such a move was seen as a dangerous, open-ended commitment—Iran might fail to gain a victory. In addition, it would have been a risky undertaking for the regime when oil prices were low, as they were in 1998, and thus would not have been a popular war.

For the IRGC, on the other hand, the situation in Afghanistan has a direct bearing on the health of the Islamic Republic. The IRGC favored at least a punitive strike in Afghanistan in response to the killing of Iranian diplomats in 1988. The Taliban's repression of the Shi'a is a challenge to the IRGC's role as defender of the faithful, and its support of anti-regime radicals challenges the IRGC's mandate to protect the revolution. The IRGC, charged with reducing and eventually eliminating the opium trade from Afghanistan, holds the Taliban directly responsible for the opium trade and its impact on Iranian society, which is devastating the youth (with some estimates in excess of 2 million young addicts in Iran).

The IRGC is engaged in almost daily shoot-outs with smugglers from Afghanistan and is taking heavy casualties, perhaps as many as a few hundred a year. Its response has been to bid for more military hardware and better monitoring and intelligence-gathering equipment. It has been active in the barrier- and fence-building programs on the Iran-Afghanistan border. The IRGC is also concerned about the Taliban's smuggling of arms into Iran and its support for anti-Iran

---

[21]*Tehran Times,* September 22, 1998.

terrorist groups.  The IRGC is probably involved in the transfer of arms and money to anti-Taliban groups.

The MOIS's core activities have been to observe the Taliban, to aid the anti-Taliban forces in the north, and to monitor Taliban-Pakistan links.  Little more is known of the MOIS's operations in Afghanistan, but the MOIS does fulfill an important anti-sabotage role in eastern Iran, where the Taliban have been active and where it is possible that the MKO has been able to infiltrate through Afghanistan.  The MOIS probably is involved in facilitating the transfer of arms to anti-Taliban Afghan groups in the north.

## Pakistan

Pakistan and Iran have long had close relations, but the health of this relationship is declining.  During the Cold War, both countries feared the growth of Moscow's power in the region and backed different anti-Soviet groups in Afghanistan.  The regular armed forces of both countries have long maintained good working relationships, and the defense establishments have conducted limited joint research.

In recent years, these strong ties have begun to fray.  Afghanistan has gone from a source of unity to an issue of contention.  Pakistan's recent nuclear sabre rattling also highlighted for Iran its own relative weakness regarding WMD.  Elements within the IRGC openly worry about Pakistan's support for the Taliban.  Iran also blamed Pakistan for the death of Iranian diplomats in Afghanistan in August 1998.[22] In addition, as anti-Shi'a violence in Pakistan has escalated in recent years, fears are growing that Pakistan may become virulently anti-Shi'a.  Many forces in Islamabad, particularly its security establishment, have forged close ties with anti-Shi'a forces in Saudi Arabia.  Pakistan's Shi'a community feels threatened by the prospective introduction of Sharia law.  If sectarian incidents continue, an exodus of the Shi'a community seems likely.[23]

---

[22]Buchta, *Who Rules Iran?* p. 147.

[23]Farhan Bokari, "Pakistan's Shias Live in Fear of Further Massacres," *Financial Times*, January 11, 1999.

Even more worrying for Iranian security agencies has been the Pakistani government's inability to rein in anti-Iranian activities. Such acts as the 1999 murder of an Iranian diplomat in Multan, the attack on Iran's cultural center in Lahore in 1997, and the murder of five IRGC officers in Rawalpindi in September 1997 have forced the Iranian security forces to develop a more concerned line on Pakistan.

## Agendas of Iran's Security Institutions

The *Artesh* is keen to contain problems with Islamabad and capitalize on the existing relationship between the two countries' armed forces in order to strengthen Iran's R&D efforts in military fields. Furthermore, *Artesh* commanders are not yet convinced that Pakistan poses a direct threat to Iran and its regional interests. The *Artesh* does, however, worry about the security fallout of the nuclear arms race in the Indian subcontinent. Officers have said in private that Iran may have little option but to develop its own nuclear option as a deterrent.

The IRGC is more concerned about Pakistan's politico-military role in the area. First, there is the continuing violence against the Shi'a community there. The IRGC sees it as its mission to provide some protection for this minority. Second, the IRGC, along with the MOIS, monitors the links between the Pakistani intelligence services and the Taliban. The IRGC and MOIS have also been known to wage counterintelligence operations against the Pakistan-based MKO and even to engage in murders of its members there. In recent years, though, this aspect of their operations in Pakistan has been less significant.

The anti-Iranian activities in particular could lead to an increase in tension. The fear of the *Artesh* is that murders in Pakistan will lead to an escalation of tensions between the two neighbors and may force conventionally armed Iran to challenge its nuclear neighbor for the first time. At the other end of the scale, the IRGC has wanted revenge for these deaths.

## The Gulf States

Since the revolution, Iran's relations with Saudi Arabia and the traditional Arab sheikdoms of the Persian Gulf have been troubled at best. Immediately after the revolution, Iran sought to export its Islamist revolutionary model to the Gulf states. Tehran denounced Gulf leaders as corrupt apostates and backed Shi'a radicals in the Gulf states. In the late 1980s and early 1990s, even as its revolutionary ardor waned, Iran still competed with Saudi Arabia for leadership of the Muslim world. Iran forged ties to Sunni Muslim radicals, whom the Gulf states viewed as a grave threat.

Since 1996, however, Iran has courted the Gulf states with some success. Saudi Arabia has been Tehran's primary target. The two countries' defense ministers have met several times, and Iranian naval vessels have visited the Saudi Red Sea port of Jeddah. Iran has also sought to improve its relations with Oman, Qatar, and Kuwait. The Iranian military has been planning joint exercises with its Gulf Cooperation Council (GCC) neighbors, area military commanders have visited one another's capitals, and Iran has announced plans for confidence-building measures in the Gulf.[24]

The warming of relations between Iran and Saudi Arabia is indicative of a genuine pragmatism on the part of Iran. Even a few years ago, the possibility of a rapprochement appeared remote.[25] Iran has had to soften its claims to Muslim leadership and its campaign against Saudi Arabia's "corrupt" and "American" Islam. Iran has curbed its rivalry with the Saudis to the extent of relinquishing its customary practice of staging demonstrations during the Hajj. Moreover, Iran has made sure that its opposition to the Taliban did not affect its rapprochement with Saudi Arabia, which has often favored the Taliban.

---

[24]For example, the commander of the Iranian navy, Admiral Abbas Mohtaj, observed that Iran and Oman had already sent delegations to monitor each other's exercises and looked to others to follow suit. *IRNA* (Tehran, in English), September 4, 1999, BBC ME/3632 MED/13, September 6, 1999.

[25]Shahram Chubin and Charles Tripp, "Iran-Saudi Relations and Regional Order," *Adelphi Paper*, no. 304 (London: IISS, 1996).

Iran's improved relations have borne fruit. Saudi Arabia and Iran, to the surprise of many observers, have cooperated with regard to oil production in OPEC, with little or no cheating. Tehran also seeks to cool the UAE's hostility regarding mutual claims to Abu Musa and the Tunb Islands, working with the other Gulf states to isolate the UAE. In practice, Iran has abandoned its demands that the Gulf states stop supporting Western troops and is now seeking to use military cooperation to reassure the Gulf states.

The rapprochement with Saudi Arabia and the other Gulf states exemplifies the increasing importance of economics in Iran's foreign policy. The need to improve coordination in OPEC in the face of declining oil prices overcame Iran's religious and nationalist convictions. Iran has been able to reverse its policies in the Gulf without serious internal opposition or dissent, which suggests that most elites recognize the need for better relations with the Gulf states.

Iran shares several other interests with the GCC states that contribute to better relations. Iran, like Kuwait and Saudi Arabia, sees Saddam's Iraq as aggressive and highly dangerous. Both Iran and the GCC states seek stability of the waterway to ensure the flow of oil. Iran also wants to exploit and manage the resources of the region when feasible. Thus, it supplies water to Qatar and is working with it to develop their shared natural gas reserves.

Relations are not harmonious in all areas. Tehran is troubled by the close ties the Gulf states have to Washington and their support for the U.S. military presence in the region. More generally, Iran seeks to be recognized as the preeminent regional power—a goal in keeping with its nationalist ambitions. To this end, it wants the Gulf states to respect its wishes and interests. In the past, it also has pursued its claim to Abu Musa and the Tunb Islands aggressively, even though these are also claimed by the UAE.

Tehran still regards Saudi Arabia as an ideological rival, in Central Asia and in west Asia, and as a close ally of the United States. Riyadh is conscious of the latent threat Iran poses to its interests in the Persian Gulf and beyond, but is more keen at present to develop the friendship with the pragmatic Iranian leadership and carve for itself the role of a mediator in Iranian-American exploratory discussions.

## *Agendas of Iran's Security Institutions*

The *Artesh* has welcomed better relations with Saudi Arabia and has pushed an agenda of confidence-building measures. The *Artesh* has worked with Iran's Foreign Ministry to ensure that its voice is heard. Since 1997, this strategy has been the dominant line out of Tehran. Military realism, designed to reduce tensions, explains the high-level military exchanges between Tehran and Riyadh and the less hostile posture that the Iranian navy has been adopting toward the U.S. Fifth Fleet in recent years.

Minister of Defense Admiral Ali Shamkhani has championed improved relations with the GCC states as an effective way of blunting the United States' political attacks on Iran and removing any pretexts for U.S. intervention against Iran, or indeed the continuing military presence in the Persian Gulf.[26] He and his *Artesh* advisors have been instrumental in the development of military ties with Oman, going as far as engaging in token exercises and joint patrolling of the Straits of Hormuz.[27]

The *Artesh* seeks to detach its dispute with the UAE over Abu Musa and the Tunb Islands from its broader relations with the Gulf states. The *Artesh* is of the view that it has to defend the disputed three islands as part of Iranian territory, making it unlikely that the country can reach a satisfactory accommodation with the UAE. The *Artesh* does not, however, want to see its show of force or government intransigence leading to an open confrontation with the UAE and the GCC, which could invite the U.S. Fifth Fleet to take up position against Iran.

------

[26]Shamkhani's calls for new Persian Gulf security arrangements have been adopted by the political leadership and been built on by the Khatami administration. It was Shamkhani who said in 1997 that the Persian Gulf littoral states "should seriously opt for formulation of a stable and coordinated strategy to reach sustainable security without foreign involvement." *Ettela'at International*, January 9, 1997.

[27]The *Artesh*'s enthusiasm for a collective security pact in the Persian Gulf and the lengths it is prepared to go to make this Iran's declared Gulf policy were again highlighted in May 1999, during the official visit of Prince Sultan Bin Abdul Aziz, Saudi Arabia's Defense Minister, to Tehran. Upon Prince Sultan's arrival at Mehrabad airport, Shamkhani broke protocol, entering into a one-to-one exchange with the prince in which he pushed the Persian Gulf collective security issue before his political masters had had the chance to enter into any discussions with the prince.

The IRGC has been told by Iran's senior political leadership to reduce its support for anti-regime Shi'a groups in the GCC, as is evident from the apparent withdrawal of Iranian support for the Bahraini opposition. The MOIS, likewise, has a minor role to play in the GCC context, except, wherever it can, to monitor the activities of Western personnel and the Iranian community in these countries.

The IRGC, however, has played a leading role in preparing for contingencies against the United States. It has developed a denial doctrine, procuring weapons systems and training its forces as part of an overall strategy to deter the United States from anti-Iranian actions and, if necessary, impose costs on U.S. forces if they choose a confrontation. The *Artesh* contributes to these efforts.

## Central Asia and the Caucasus

The collapse of the Soviet Union offered tremendous potential benefits to Iran. Tehran looked at the newfound independence of the states in the north as a diplomatic opportunity to break out of the containment imposed by the United States. Iran has cultural and historical ties with the Caucasian states to its northwest and the Central Asian states to its northeast (none more so than Persian-speaking Tajikistan). Furthermore, it shares with these states an interest in nurturing their independence from Russia.

Geography favors Iran. Most of these states are landlocked. Azerbaijan, Turkmenistan, and Kazakhstan have access to the Caspian, but this is a closed, inland sea. Quite apart from trade with Iran, gaining access to the open waters of the south is important to these states for securing markets in the Middle East and beyond. Iran's natural link from the Caspian to the Gulf and, through it, to the Indian Ocean thus constitutes a potentially important asset for Iran in its relations with these states. Iran's own economy stands to benefit from such relations, from the viewpoint not just of transit fees or even swap arrangements but also of markets for goods that Iran itself produces.[28]

---

[28]Amir Houshang Amini, "Iran's Standing in the Regional Geo-Economic Equation," *Iran Commerce* (Iran Chamber of Commerce, Industries and Mines), vol. 4, no. 2, Autumn 1997, pp. 20-24.

As a result of poor relations with the United States, however, few of these potential advantages have been realized. U.S. sanctions, pressure against projects with Iran, and inducements for alternative schemes have closed this avenue for Iran's economic development. Given the parlous state of Iran's economy, finding ways to benefit from this area is likely to remain a priority.

The Caspian itself is an issue, both of cooperation and of rivalry. Iran, like Russia, seeks a share of Caspian resources greater than the share it is entitled to based on its coastline. Tehran also seeks regional stability to encourage trade and the development of resources. In addition, the Caspian is an important training base for Iran's navy.

### Concerns About Communal Unrest

This enthusiasm for the economic opportunities Central Asia offers is tempered in practice by a real conservatism with regard to existing borders and support for the rights of minorities. In general, Tehran has sought stability. When conflict has arisen, Iran's preferred stance has been as mediator, offering its good offices and suggesting peace formulas. It has sought (not always successfully) to avoid identification with one side.[29] Tehran fears that the disintegration of neighboring states and the assertiveness of their ethnic groups could create models for Iran's own potentially restive communities. Given the location of Iran's minorities on its periphery and adjacent to these areas, the risks of spillover and imitation would be profound. Hence, Iran has eschewed opportunism or activism:

- In June 1989, on a visit to the USSR, President Rafsanjani advised Azerbaijan to stay within the USSR.

- Iran, in contrast to Turkey, reluctantly and belatedly recognized the breakup of the USSR.

---

[29]See inter alia the articles of: Hanna Yousif Freij, "State Interest vs. the Umma: Iranian Policy in Central Asia," *Middle East Journal*, vol. 50, no. 1, Winter 1996, pp. 71-83; Adam Tarock, "Iran's Policy in Central Asia," *Central Asian Survey*, vol. 16, no. 2, 1997, pp. 185-200; Mohiaddin Mesbahi, "Tajikistan, Iran and the International Politics of the 'Islamic Factor,'" *Central Asian Survey*, vol. 16, no. 2, 1997, pp. 141-158. See also, "Iran's Relations with the States of Central Asia and Transcaucasia," *Background Brief* (London: Foreign and Commonwealth Office, August 1998).

- In Persian-speaking Tajikistan, Iran offered a formula for peace based on the inclusion of all factions, despite its cultural ties and the strength of the Islamist movement there.

- Iran has worked closely with Christian Armenia, supporting it tacitly in its conflict with Shi'a Muslim Azerbaijan.

- During Russia's wars with Muslim Chechnya, Iran referred to the matter as an "internal" issue.

Azerbaijan has great potential to destabilize Iran, but both governments have adopted cautious and pragmatic policies toward each other. Even though there is little support for Azeri separatism in Iran, Tehran is particularly sensitive to any threat to its ethnic harmony and has sought the extradition of Iranian Azeri separatists from Baku. Fortunately for Iran, there is little evidence that Baku seeks to promote unification of the two Azerbaijans. Iranian Azeri separatist inclinations are limited and dormant. Groups such as the New Union Organization, headed by Mohammed Ali Galibi, do not appear to enjoy mass support. Preoccupied with unstable politics, a succession problem, the conflict with Armenia, and pipeline politics, Azerbaijan cultivates Iranian support. This fits in with Iran's priorities—to emphasize state-to-state relations and common interests.[30]

Given the instability in the region, Iran has both mediated disputes and used its muscle to prevent any dramatic change in the status quo. Iran has tried to mediate the Nagarno Karabakh dispute, but when Azerbaijan was threatened by an Armenian offensive in mid-1993, which produced a steady stream of refugees across the Iranian border, Iran threatened Armenia with direct intervention. For Iran, balancing rather than taking sides is not always easy. Domestic politics and Pan-Shi'a sympathy argued for a tilt in favor of the Azeris. Pragmatic national interest, however, argued for an approach that left Iran with influence with Armenian, particularly as Turkey has favored Baku.

---

[30]President Khatami, after referring to the common historical, religious, and cultural bonds shared by the two countries, observed: "What's important is that the fates of the two countries are linked together." Mohammed Khatami, *IRNA*, December 1, 1998.

Iran has cultivated Turkmenistan, with which it shares a border of 1,500 kilometers.[31] A friendship treaty was signed in 1992. In 1996, the Bandar Abbas-Tedzhen railway line opened communications between Turkmenistan and other Central Asian states and Iran and Turkey. Border trade is growing. Iran's Turkoman population shows no sign of restiveness or a desire to link up with their nomadic cousins of the north.

## Agendas of Iran's Security Institutions

Neither the *Artesh* nor the IRGC focuses considerable attention on Central Asia or the Caucasus. The *Artesh* does monitor the Afghani-Tajik border and the flow of arms to pro-Taliban forces in Central Asia. It has not developed a coherent policy toward instability in Central Asia and, since the departure of the Kazakh nuclear warheads, does not regard Central Asian states as major threats to Iran. The *Artesh* has been directed to strategize about a possible joint American-Turkish–sponsored military move into Central Asia and the use of Central Asian territories as launching pads for operations against Iran. It is not known how the *Artesh*'s strategic thinking on these matters has been unfolding. The IRGC and MOIS have an almost invisible role there and, since the Tajik civil war in the early 1990s, have not been engaged in any known operations there.

Three issues underpin the *Artesh*'s thinking about Azerbaijan and Armenia: the danger that renewed fighting will lead to an influx of refugees to Iran, increased outside involvement in the area, and concern about the militarization of the Caspian as a consequence of oil exploration. The *Artesh*, already preparing a strategy for development of Iran's naval presence and facilities in the Caspian, is anxious to portray these moves as defensive measures designed to protect Iran's Caspian interests. The Turkish-Israeli dimension rears its head here as well, as the *Artesh*'s political masters see the two countries bolstering Azerbaijan's position vis-à-vis Iran.

---

[31]Turkmenistan is a desert fiefdom of 5 million run by an authoritarian ruler. There are 800,000 Turkomans in the northeastern Iranian province of Khorasan. Turkmenistan has proclaimed itself officially neutral. It remains poor and landlocked, with its potential wealth from gas so far unrealized. Turkmenistan's political development matches its economy, which is archaic and primitive.

Neither the IRGC nor the MOIS plays a prominent role with relation to Azerbaijan and Armenia. The IRGC seeks to win over the sympathies of its only Shi'a-dominated neighbor, but the regime limits the scope of its activities. The MOIS's interest is in containing any separatist campaigns across the border in Iranian Azerbaijan. Neither, however, is willing to challenge the existing tilt toward Yerevan.

## Syria and Lebanon

Iran and Syria have close relations that are entirely geostrategic in origin. For the two decades after the revolution, both nations shunned the West, rejected peace with Israel, and opposed Saddam Hussein's regime in Baghdad. Moreover, the 'Alawi regime in Syria is anathema to Sunni radicals, as is Iran's Shi'a regime. Both countries sought to use Lebanon's Shi'a population to harass Israel. While almost the entire Arab world supported Iraq in its war with Iran, Damascus sided with Tehran.

Iran's relations with Lebanon have long been close, if unusual. In contrast to its course in the states along its border, Tehran has long worked at a subnational level in Lebanon and has fostered instability in the country. In 1982, Iran deployed a 1,500-man contingent of the IRGC to Baalbak in Lebanon that helped organize, train, supply, and support Hezballah.[32] Many Lebanese Shi'a religious leaders studied in Iran. Indeed, an older generation of religious leaders of both countries studied in theological seminars in Iraq.

Iran has cut back its support for Hezballah, but ties remain strong. In the 1990s, the IRGC's presence was cut to roughly 150 fighters. Hezballah, for its part, has moved away from parroting the line of the Iranian government and focuses far more on the narrower concerns of Lebanon's Shi'a community. Since 1992, Hezballah has participated in Lebanon's parliamentary politics, further leading the movement to moderate its agenda. Hezballah's leaders have also refrained from recognizing Ayatollah Khamene'i as their source of

---

[32]Augustus Richard Norton, "Walking Between Raindrops: Hizballah in Lebanon," *Mediterranean Politics*, vol. 3, no. 1, Summer 1998, p. 86.

emulation, further straining ties.[33]  Iran, however, continues to arm Hezballah and encourages it to maintain a significant military capability.

So far, Iranian and Syrian interests have operated in relative harmony, but Iran's policy toward Lebanon will depend heavily on the status of Syrian-Israeli relations.  The impact of the Israeli withdrawal from southern Lebanon remains unclear.  Iran's initial response was to send officials to try to preserve its influence over Hezballah's agenda.  Many Hezballah members, however, probably have little enthusiasm for cross-border attacks into Israel.[34]

### Agendas of Iran's Security Institutions

In contrast to most of Iran's important relationships, in the case of Lebanon, the IRGC, rather than the *Artesh*, has more influence on the agenda.  *Artesh* leaders see the involvement in Lebanon as offering few benefits to Iran, particularly now that Israel has withdrawn. They question the resources devoted to Lebanon, which they believe could be better used for other purposes.  *Artesh* officials are enthusiastic about ties to Syria, which they see as necessary to balance Iraq and Israel.

However, the IRGC is committed to maintaining influence in Lebanon, perhaps more than in any other country.  Many IRGC officials, having acted as midwife for Hezballah, believe that its success is in large part due to Iran's efforts.  Yet even the IRGC has tempered its ambitions regarding Lebanon.  Most officials appear content with Hezballah influence in the country and recognize that an Islamic state along the Iranian model is not likely.

The IRGC regards its presence in Lebanon as having been a great success for Iran and is keen to learn from this experience.  It sees its Lebanon presence as providing it with the expertise to provide guidance in other circumstances where it could play an active role in training, educating, and motivating Shi'as under siege.  The IRGC has

---

[33]Norton, "Walking Between Raindrops," pp. 86-100. See also Magnus Ranstorp, "The Strategy and Tactics of Hizballah's Current 'Lebanonization Process,'" *Mediterranean Politics*, vol. 3, no. 1, Summer 1998, p. 118.

[34]Norton, "Walking Between Raindrops," p. 99.

tried, and will try again, to apply lessons learned in Lebanon to some of the problems of Shi'as in other beleaguered countries.

## Israel

Israel and its over-the-horizon ally, the United States, take up much of the national security debate in Iran.  The rhetoric is constant. Supreme Leader Khamene'i's recent call for the "annihilation" of Israel is typical rather than exceptional.[35]  With regard to Israel, there is almost universal agreement that the Jewish state is an active regional rival bent on checking Iran's political and military power and undoing Iran's achievements.[36]  Military leaders and their political masters seem to be convinced that Israel is planning a confrontation with Iran.  Thus, as Israeli diplomacy and economic force reach the shores of the Persian Gulf and the Caspian Sea, Tehran sees further concrete evidence of Israel's encirclement strategy.

For the past two decades, Islamic Iran has championed the Palestinian cause as the means to assert its claim to Muslim leadership. Iran's rejection of a diplomatic solution as necessarily adverse to Muslim interests, its depiction of the United States as the evil genius behind Israeli strategy, and its implacable opposition to any compromise have been a means for Iran to widen its support among Muslims beyond its otherwise limited Shi'a constituency.  Tehran depicts its refusal to countenance any "sellout" of Muslim rights as evidence of its moral superiority to the lackey regimes elsewhere. Iran's stance on this issue has made it the leader of the rejectionist camp and given it a certain amount of leverage as spoiler.  When the peace process is moving, Iran can move to sabotage it; when it is frozen, Tehran can point to the wisdom of withholding support from a bankrupt process.

Iran has supported Palestinian terrorist groups, for both opportunistic and ideological reasons, despite assurances from President

---

[35]Afshin Valinejad, "Iran Leader Calls for Israel's Annihilation," *Boston Globe*, January 1, 2000, p. 4.

[36]"Roundtable: New Geopolitical Developments in the Region and Iranian National Security," *Middle East Studies Quarterly* (Tehran), vol. 5, nos. 1-2, Summer and Fall 1998, pp. 5-54.

Khatami to the United States, Arafat, and others. The Palestinian authority has blamed Iran and Iranian-backed groups for bombings in Israel.[37] Several explanations for this are possible:

- Iranian and U.S. views of what constitutes a terrorist group differ.

- Iran does not consider financial support of Hamas or other radical Palestinian groups irresponsible or out of bounds, perhaps because the Gulf states and their citizens provide considerable support for these groups with little public U.S. criticism.

- Khatami may not yet be in a position to control all aspects of policy or all arms of his decentralized government. Militant groups may report to the IRGC and the Iranian ambassador in Lebanon and bypass the president. More likely, as the discussion below indicates, Khatami is aware of militant group activities and exercises some control over them.

- Some Iranian leaders prefer to use this issue as leverage against the United States.

- Iran does not believe that the United States can find a "smoking gun" that will link it directly to those who commit terrorist acts. By working through front groups or the Lebanese Hezballah, Iran seeks to maintain denial of responsibility.

Relations with Palestinian groups, however, are lukewarm at best. Many Palestinian fundamentalists are hostile to Iran's Shi'a leadership and ideology. In addition, Palestinian groups have few illusions about the depth of Iran's commitment. This tepid relationship makes it unlikely that Iran would continue to actively champion the Palestinian cause should the Palestinians embrace peace with Israel.

Another aspect of Iran's relations with Israel is linked to Tehran-Washington relations. This stems from Iran's recognition that Washington places a high price on the success of the peace process and, indeed, cites Iran's opposition as one of the principal obstacles to normal relations. Some in the Iranian leadership clearly find continued militancy on this issue a useful way of both exerting pressure on

---

[37]Radio Free Europe/Radio Liberty, *Iran Report*, vol. 2, no. 45, December 15, 1999 (electronic version).

Washington—forcing the United States to pay a price to Iran to desist from its spoiler role—and, if that fails, preventing any normalization of relations.[38]

Iran and Israel are both highly concerned about the other's nuclear and missile programs. Israel sees Iran's potential nuclear program as one of the greatest threats to its security, particularly as Tehran has recently tested missiles that can reach Israeli territory. Many Iranians, for their part, see Israel as an implacable enemy and believe that its nuclear capability is a threat to Iran's security.

The picture is not immutable. Iran has no specific or direct dispute with Israel. Both countries are hostile to Iraq and concerned about Sunni radicalism. Under the Shah, a shared rivalry with the Arab world led to a close strategic alliance. However, no one in the defense establishment questions Iran's political line on Israel and the Arab-Israeli peace process. Some have expressed an interest in trying to find a modus vivendi with Israel, if for no other reason than to buy more time for Iran; theirs is not a very loud voice.

Iran, however, has also paid a considerable price with the United States for its high-profile rejection of the peace process. Some Iranians now ask why they should pay for the causes of others, particularly when those most concerned wish to arrive at a diplomatic settlement. Iran's leadership is thus under a certain degree of pressure internally not to get too involved or to pay too high a price for a continued role in the Arab-Israeli issue.

## Agendas of Iran's Security Institutions

All of Iran's security institutions view Israel as a hostile country with the means, power, and resources to pose a serious security threat to Iran. More broadly, the military establishment is fearful of the growing Turkish-Israeli partnership. IRGC and *Artesh* leaders have spoken out against the partnership and have warned of its conse-

---

[38]It is noteworthy that Iran became more intractable and more militant on this issue in the wake of the 1991 Gulf war, when Washington, in Tehran's view, reneged on an implied commitment to include Iran in a Gulf security arrangement. Instead, Washington froze Tehran out through dual containment; Iran's response, this view runs, was to increase support for the rejectionist front.

quences for Iran and the Arab world. Although both the IRGC and the *Artesh* favor developing a deterrent force against Israel through long-range missiles and bombers, they fear that Iran's forces will not be able to deter or defend Iran against an Israeli attack.

The IRGC's agenda toward Israel has been shaped by its long presence in Lebanon and the military aspects of the Syrian-Iranian-Hezballah triangle. The unilateral withdrawal of Israeli forces from southern Lebanon and the death of Hafez Al-Assad, however, are forcing the IRGC to rethink its support for Hezballah's attacks on Israel.

## Europe

Iran's relationship with Europe has always been better than its relationship with the United States. Many European countries maintained diplomatic ties and commercial relations with Iran even during the heady days of the revolution. Since 1992, Europe has engaged Iran in a "critical dialog," which has done little to influence Iranian behavior. Ties to Europe have warmed significantly since Khatami became president in 1997. In 1999, Khatami visited several European countries, and European leaders declared that Iran was no longer committing terrorism abroad and was cooperating on WMD issues.[39] Britain reestablished diplomatic ties at the ambassadorial level in response to Iran's rejection—only at the official level—of government support for the assassination of Salman Rushdie.

Good relations with Europe are vital for Iran's economic development. Tehran needs both investment and financial credit to shore up its troubled economy. European participation is particularly necessary given continued U.S. hostility to Iran.

Iran has sought to divide Europe from the United States by offering the Europeans access to its market, which Iranians believe is irresistible. The assumption behind this policy is that the greedy for-

_____

[39]de Bellaigue, "The Struggle for Iran," p. 57.

eigners are basically in competition, which gives Iran some leverage. The reverse side is that Iran wants to cultivate Europe (and Japan) to isolate the United States.[40]

## Agendas of Iran's Security Institutions

Relations with Europe are not a major concern for either the *Artesh* or the IRGC. Both institutions believe that European powers are no longer a force in the Middle East in general and the Persian Gulf in particular. The *Artesh*'s main interest in Europe is as a possible source of advanced weapons. As such, Iran can do business with European countries, and the armed forces may be able to benefit from broadening contacts with the core members of the European Union.[41] At present, the MOIS is more interested in monitoring the expatriate community in Europe than in masterminding any campaigns against them. This strategy is very much in keeping with the Khatami administration's foreign policy agenda and attitude toward the large expatriate community.

## The United States

In contrast to most of Iran's relationships, its ties to the United States are clouded by ideology, nationalism, and occasional paranoia. Continuing U.S. sanctions and refusal to accept Iran as a legitimate state rankle Iran's leadership. (The degree to which Iran's own actions are responsible for this is minimized.) Iran's historical grievances—U.S. support for the coup against Mosaddeq, subsequent U.S. backing of the Shah, and the long-term U.S. support for Israel—nurture its perception that the United States sided with Iraq

---

[40]Roula Khalaf, "World Bank May Resume Iran Loans," *Financial Times*, January 29/30, 2000, p. 3.

[41]Tehran's view of France as a NATO country and independent actor from the United States has fed into the military's thinking about this European country. While *Artesh* accepts that Iran has not had a close military partnership with France in the past, it hopes that it can use French expertise in military R&D, military air transport, naval technology, and upgrades of its aging missile systems.

during its war with Iran and its general sense that Washington seeks to undermine Iran.[42]

Broadly speaking, most Iranians would agree with the following criticisms of the United States:

- The United States is arrogant and bullies lesser powers. It uses its power in a discriminatory and punitive fashion.

- The United States is a cultural threat to Islamic civilization.

- The United States finds it difficult to have normal relations with states that disagree with it. Independence and good relations with the United States are often incompatible.

- U.S. policy in relation to sanctions and especially technology denial is an example of U.S. hypocrisy and unwillingness to share power with other states.[43]

- The U.S. military presence in the Persian Gulf is a provocation and should be reduced.

In general, Iran's leaders are likely to view any U.S. actions, even those intended as conciliatory gestures, with suspicion.

### Prospects for Better Relations

Iran's complaints about the United States are not shared throughout the elite. Many Iranians recognize that American help in renovating Iran's tattered oil infrastructure would be invaluable. Some argue that the U.S. presence in the Gulf is necessary to ensure the implementation of UN resolutions, the containment of Saddam's Iraq, and even the reassurance of the GCC. The utility of the United States as an enemy, the need, as it were, for a Great Satan, has diminished within Iran. Despite its efforts, the clerical leadership finds this issue without great resonance in Iran today. Official anti-Americanism,

---

[42]Jerrold D. Green, "Iran: Limits to Rapprochement," statement before the House Committee on Foreign Relations, Subcommittee on Near Eastern and South Asian Affairs, May 1999.

[43]Ali Asghar and Keivan Hosseini, "The US and the Technological Ban on Iran," *The Journal of Defence Policy* (*Siyasat–e Defa'i*), vol. 7, no. 1, Winter 1998/1999, pp. 49-68.

such as government-sponsored demonstrations to protest U.S. poli-cies, is considered by many Iranians to be almost comical. Attempts to blame the United States for the student protests in June 1999 simi-larly were seen as a transparent attempt to shift blame from the regime.

Iran's geopolitical differences with the United States are not abso-lute. Interests overlap in the Caucasus and Central Asia, Afghanistan, and even in the Gulf, regarding Iraq. Iran's quest for status need not threaten U.S. interests. Iran is not a territorially revisionist state in the Gulf or elsewhere, and Iran can live comfortably with the Gulf states.

A climate for improved relations is developing in Iran, though even reformers do not see close relations with the United States as a pri-ority.[44] Many Iranians appear to like Americans, if not U.S. govern-ment policy. The allure of American popular culture is also strong. Khatami's January 1998 interview with CNN symbolized the ability of Iranian elites to discuss, at least tentatively, the prospect of improved relations with Washington. The issue of a resumption of relations with the United States is no longer taboo, though it alarms many conservatives who feel that contact with the United States will lead to Westernization. Reportedly, Iran's senior security-making body se-cretly voted to establish ties with Washington, though Supreme Leader Khamene'i vetoed this decision.[45] Attempts by the hard-liners to prosecute reformers such as Abdullah Nouri for advocating the renewal of relations with the United States have demonstrated the degree to which the subject has escaped the control of the authorities.

## Agendas of Iran's Security Institutions

Most military commanders acknowledge the overwhelming power of the United States and caution against adventurist policies that might lead to conflict with Washington or with its regional allies. They would like to see U.S. forces leave the Persian Gulf (though they

---

[44]Gasiorowski, "The Power Struggle in Iran."

[45]Scott Peterson, "Iran Opens Door—a Little—to U.S.," *Christian Science Monitor*, February 25, 2000, p. 1.

avoid the question of whether this would allow the Iraqi threat to grow) and curtail military support for the Arab Gulf states, but they now recognize that this would happen only if Washington's GCC allies were convinced of Iran's friendship.

The *Artesh*'s perceptions of the United States are shaped by the Iranian navy's confrontation with the U.S. navy in the late 1980s and by the performance of the U.S. armed forces in the 1990-1991 Kuwait crisis. *Artesh* leaders viewed the U.S. ability to bring some 500,000 personnel to the region and quickly defeat Iraq with amazement. The large and varied U.S. presence is also viewed with concern and considered an important planning challenge.

Several current U.S. proposals also concern the *Artesh*. The *Artesh* is anxious about the U.S. military's use of over-the-horizon weapons, such as cruise missiles, and is thinking about how to counter this strength. The *Artesh* leadership also fears that the U.S. proposal for the extension of a defensive shield around the GCC states would challenge Iran's defense and security capabilities and embolden the Gulf states to take a less conciliatory line toward Iran.

The *Artesh* seeks to avoid any direct confrontation with U.S. forces in the Persian Gulf. Some *Artesh* leaders recognize the role the United States plays in containing Iraq. In addition, some leaders recall the greater status and strength the *Artesh* enjoyed during the days of the Shah, when it cooperated closely with the U.S. military.

The *Artesh*, however, is also hedging against a possible confrontation by trying to create a credible deterrent against the U.S. navy, by deploying (or helping the IRGC to deploy) anti-ship systems, radar, and new platforms for aggressive maneuvers in the Gulf. The military forces' strategy seems to be based on raising the cost to the United States of naval operations against Iranian forces. Iran's armed forces would aim to do this through a strategy of denial, where they would blockade the Straits of Hormuz and engage in naval operations to harass the U.S. Fifth Fleet.[46] Iran would probably also target the installations of U.S. oil companies in the Gulf. Since the Khobar Towers bombing in 1996, the military establishment as a whole has been on

---

[46]*Iran News*, April 28, 1997.

higher alert, where the political leadership has openly talked of a possible revenge U.S. attack on Iran.

The IRGC's agenda toward the United States is more ideological than practical. It sees the United States as heading a cultural invasion of the country and responds to the elite's desire to combat this invasion. The IRGC, however, also regards the United States as a military threat. As Brigadier General Baqr Zolqadr, deputy IRGC commander, has put it: "Today, the United States is the only enemy we take as a main threat in our strategy. None of the regional countries are at a level to be a threat against Iran's security. We have organized our forces and equipment to counter the U.S. threats, and our exercises and maneuvers have been arranged on the basis of these threats."[47] The *Artesh*, however, tries to restrict the IRGC's actions in the Gulf, preventing it from challenging the U.S. naval presence in an open fashion and trying to limit the IRGC's sphere of operations during exercises.

### Impact of U.S. Policies on Iran's Military

Washington's "dual containment" policy has hampered the Iranian military's drive to develop its armed forces but has not stopped it altogether. Washington's impact is best understood by recognizing what has not occurred. Western states, which in general produce the most sophisticated military equipment, have hesitated to sell arms to the clerical regime. The United States has also used its diplomatic and economic muscle to prevent or curtail sales by China and Russia to Iran. As a result, Iran's forces have poor equipment, which is often not interoperable, and receive little training. Nevertheless, Tehran has been able to secure some arms deals, technology transfers, and training from these sources, with a primary constraint on its purchases being financial.

U.S. policies and rhetoric have strengthened the position of the military in Iran. The anti-Iran vitriol common in some Washington circles, the establishment of the U.S. Fifth Fleet in the Persian Gulf, U.S. military exercises with Iran's GCC allies, and U.S. Central Command (CENTCOM) military planning changes have all tended to strengthen

---

[47]*Kayhan*, December 10, 1996.

the hand of the military establishment and its relations with the political elite. The extension of CENTCOM's Area of Responsibility north of the Iranian border to Central Asia, particularly when combined with NATO discussions with states in the Caucasus, contributes to the perception that the United States is trying to squeeze Iran and prevent it from exercising its proper influence in the region.

## KEY TRANSNATIONAL ISSUES

Iran's policies on cross-regional issues, such as support for coreligionists abroad and their attempts to proliferate, are shaped by the domestic factors, international context, and security institutions of the specific countries.

### Support for Islamic Radicals

Iran's once-close relations with Islamist movements around the world have been declining in both their scope and their scale in recent years. After the Islamic revolution, Tehran actively supported radical groups, particularly radical Shi'as, in many Muslim countries. In Iraq, Lebanon, Bahrain, Saudi Arabia, Afghanistan, and elsewhere, Iran helped organize radical Shi'a groups, encouraged them to fight against their governments, and at times armed and trained them. Tehran forged particularly close ties to the Lebanese Hezballah. After the Persian Gulf war, Iran also stepped up ties to radical Sunni groups. Playing on growing disgruntlement toward the United States, Tehran established ties and provided limited financial support to Hamas, Palestine Islamic Jihad, and other radical Sunni movements.

In recent years, however, Tehran has become less active in its support for radical Islamists. The fate of Shi'a communities outside Iran is no longer a major concern of Iran's leadership. Tehran rarely plays the Islamic card in Central Asia and has thrown its lot in with the anti-Taliban Northern Alliance in Afghanistan. In the Arab world, contacts with the Islamists remain, particularly in Lebanon and with pro-Syrian Palestinian groups. Tehran has cut ties, or at least reduced the visibility of relations with, Islamic radicals in the GCC, Egypt, Jordan, Sudan, and North Africa.[48] With regard to Iraq, Iran maintains an active Islamist front based in Iran. Yet even here it has not exploited much of the civil unrest to the degree that outside analysts expected.

Iran's ties to radical Palestinian groups, however, remain strong and may be growing stronger. Iran has stepped up shipments of weapons to Hamas in recent years. Ties to Hamas have grown in part because U.S. pressure has led supporters in Arab countries, particularly in the Persian Gulf, to reduce their contributions, making Hamas more willing to work with Tehran. Tehran has also coordinated groups working against Israel. Thus, it has trained Hamas and Hezballah members in Iran and in Lebanon, in cooperation with the Popular Front for the Liberation of Palestine–General Command, a small but extremely violent Palestinian rejectionist group.[49]

Pakistan has suffered an increase in Iranian-backed subversion and terrorism. The oppression and brutalization of Pakistan's Shi'a community may have inspired Iran to become more active. Moreover, as the West evinces little interest in the violence in Pakistan, Iran's activities there do little to harm its image.[50]

In general, arguments that Iran's support for terrorism occurs without official sanction and without the knowledge of the senior leadership have proven incorrect. Terrorist acts overseas usually require the coordination of various government ministries and revolutionary organizations, coordination that would be difficult without support from Iran's senior leadership.[51] In 1997, a German court ruled that the murder of four Iranian Kurdish opposition figures in a café in Berlin in 1992 was authorized by a committee that included Iran's

---

[48]See "Iran: Wrapping Up the Networks?" *Gulf States Newsletter*, vol. 25, no. 629, February 7, 2000, p. 2, for an optimistic report of Iran's reduced support for radicalism in the Gulf.

[49]John Lancaster, "U.S.: Iran's Terrorism Role Grows," *Washington Post*, December 4, 1999, p. 1 (electronic version).

[50]Michael Eisenstadt, "Dilemmas for the U.S. and Iran," *Policywatch*, no. 414, October 8, 1999 (electronic version).

[51]Eisenstadt, "Dilemmas for the U.S. and Iran."

Supreme Leader, President, and Intelligence and Foreign Ministers, among others.

## Agendas of Iran's Security Institutions

The IRGC is the party most actively engaged in the defense of the Shi'a communities outside Iran.  Because it sees the Shi'as of Afghanistan, Iraq, and Pakistan as most endangered and beleaguered, it is actively engaged in providing material support for them, including training wherever necessary.  In all three cases, however, the military establishment believes that Iran's interests can best be served through the adoption of those policies that can help to ensure the territorial integrity of these countries.  Iran's role, therefore, with regard to its coreligionists in these crisis countries can best be summed up as defensive diplomacy.

Although relations with most GCC states, particularly Saudi Arabia, have improved dramatically in recent years, the IRGC retains an interest in the Shi'a communities of Bahrain, Kuwait, and Saudi Arabia, as well as in the Iranian émigré population in the UAE.  At present, the IRGC does not seem to be pursuing a disruptive or rear-guard action in relation to Iran's coreligionists in the Persian Gulf region.  Nevertheless, it almost certainly maintains ties to a range of groups and could reactivate a network if necessary.

## Commitment to WMD and Missiles

Almost all Iranian leaders see the possession of long-range missiles as vital for Iran's security.  Missiles have certain advantages over aircraft for Iran today.  Lacking access to spare parts from the West, Iran must turn to Russia or China for advanced aircraft.  China's aircraft, however, are often of poor quality and of limited sophistication.  While Russia possesses state-of-the-art aircraft, it requires Iran to train on Soviet systems rather than on Western ones, to which Iran's air force is accustomed.  Moreover, advanced aircraft are costly and need constant support—a particularly daunting problem when the supplier's reliability is in doubt.

In contrast, missiles are relatively easy to manufacture domestically, which helps Iran meet its goal of self-reliance.  What they lack in flexibility (for example, recalling them once in flight or reusing them) they make up for in their relatively low cost, their ease of conceal-ment, the assurance of penetration, and the lack of the need to train pilots. Both the *Artesh* and the IRGC see missiles as useful for deterring Israel from attacking Iran or even those countries friendly with Iran. Missiles also are high-prestige items that demonstrate Iran's technical sophistication.

Missiles, however, raise a number of issues:

- Because missiles are conventionally armed, largely inaccurate, and carry a relatively small payload, their only useful function, many argue, is as terror weapons, attacking enemy population centers in the event of a crisis. However, missiles are particularly valuable because they can deliver WMD.

- Emphasis on missiles may prompt a response from Iran's rivals, given their virtually assured penetration, and especially as Iran develops longer-range missiles. Israel is likely to be alarmed, for instance. Because of Israel's historical experience and its sensi-tivity to civilian casualties, it will have to treat any oncoming missiles *as if* they had WMD warheads.

- The use of missiles for the most ordinary contingencies (for ex-ample, Iran's use against MKO camps in Iraq in mid-1999) can reduce any general barriers to their use in the region.

Many of the reasons that might lead Iran to seek long-range missiles also give it incentives to seek WMD. Iran is seeking to develop its nuclear infrastructure in order to design and produce nuclear weapons—a goal shared widely among Iran's current elite.[52]

Iran seeks WMD for several reasons. First, Iran has plausible geopo-litical reasons for a nuclear weapons option. Iraq's intentions and behavior are by no means predictable, particularly if sanctions are lifted. Even a post-Saddam Iraq may be hostile to Iran. Pakistan and India and uncertainties about the evolution of the states in the Cau-

---

[52]Seth Carus and Michael Eisenstadt, "Iran's Nuclear Weapons Program: Status and Implications," *Policywatch*, no. 444, March 8, 2000 (electronic version).

casus and Central Asia provide other causes for concern.[53] Second, WMD—particularly nuclear weapons—are a guarantee of status, forcing states to pay attention to Iran and treat it as an equal. Third, WMD serve as equalizers, diminishing the gap between the military capabilities of weak states such as Iran and the advanced military capabilities of states such as the United States and Israel. Fourth, as noted above, WMD maximize the impact of Iran's missile forces. There is no sign, however, that Iran has made the acquisition of a nuclear capability an urgent priority.[54]

*Artesh* leaders believe Iran does not immediately need WMD but that it should have the technology and know-how for developing various types of WMD, particularly nuclear weapons. The *Artesh* and its logistics division continue to explore the potential of know-how and expertise from Russia, Ukraine, and other former Soviet republics in such fields.[55] In conversation, retired officers speak of the geopolitical tensions surrounding Iran and say that to be able to deter aggression and contain threats to its security, Iran should pursue the nuclear option. Serving officers and other officials maintain the government line that Iran will not follow the nuclear path.

The IRGC's position on WMD is more ideological and rooted in its rather political understanding of national security. It does not necessarily rule out deployment of nonconventional weapons if Iran is threatened by the same—as it already is by Iraq and Israel. Elements within the IRGC still oppose Iran's full compliance with international arms control regimes. The commander of the IRGC, Yahya Rahim Safavi, for instance, who was selected by President Khatami himself, declared at a heated meeting of the Supreme Council for National Security (SCNS): "Is it possible to stop the U.S. threats and domination goals by the policy of détente? Is it possible to save the Islamic Republic from threat of the U.S. and international Zionism by concluding agreements for prohibiting chemical and nuclear weapons

---

[53]See, for example, "India's Emerging Nuclear Threat to Persian Gulf Security," *Iranfile*, vol. 1, no. 5, February/March 1999, pp. 8-9.

[54]Nor is there a clear or enunciated notion of what use nuclear weapons would have in Iran's overall strategic doctrine. This is not surprising, as Iran is not permitted, and denies seeking, nuclear weapons.

[55]Douglas Jehl, "Rage Rises in Iran over Killing," *International Herald Tribune*, September 12, 1998, p. 9.

and international conventions?"[56]  His own answer to these questions was an emphatic no, advocating that Iran should defend its independence and revolution by any means possible and leave its WMD options open.

The limits of the security institutions' influence are suggested by Iran's ratification of the Chemical Weapons Convention (CWC).  In the run-up to Iran's submission of information to the Technical Secretariat of the Convention in November 1998, reports circulated that the *Artesh* and the IRGC had argued against full ratification without assurances that Iran's neighbors would follow its example. These objections were overruled by the SCNS.  During the inspector team's visit to the country in 1999, Iran chose to destroy some of its known chemical weapons facilities in front of the visiting team. Iran's decision to portray itself as complying with the CWC was based on its risk assessment about deployment of chemical weapons in the region and on its decision that maintaining the option would be a risky alternative.  Outright noncompliance would inevitably increase proliferation and add to Iran's national security threats.  Its show of compliance may also reflect confidence in Iran's ability to conceal its weapons programs and deceive the international community.

---

[56]*Jameah*, April 29, 1998.

# Chapter Seven

# IMPLICATIONS

The foregoing discussion suggests that Iran's security strategy stems from a complicated mix of strategic, domestic, and institutional sources. Any assessment of how Iran will respond in a crisis must determine not only the particulars, but also the current balance of influence among Tehran's decisionmakers.

Several observations of Iran's security policy can be derived.

## FOREIGN AND SECURITY POLICIES CANNOT BE SEPARATED

A distinction is often drawn among internal security, the preservation of the revolution, and Iran's broad foreign policy aims. Closer examination, however, reveals this distinction is at best blurry and at worst dangerously misleading. All of Iran's major policy decisions— how to ensure security against Iraq, whether to improve relations with Washington, how much support should be given to the anti-Israel effort, and so on—involve a complex calculus of Iran's overall vulnerability, the need to ensure the regime is strong, and Iran's commitment to revolutionary ideals.

Over the years, the balance of these influences has shifted. The ardor that characterized Iran's foreign policy in the early 1980s is gone. However, ideology continues to play an important role, particularly with regard to the United States and Israel. Similarly, although the revolution is no longer directly threatened by enemies at home and abroad as it was in the early 1980s, the regime takes any threat of internal unrest seriously. Tehran is often willing to sacrifice other long-term foreign policy objectives to silence or intimidate regime opponents.

## THE ISLAMIC REPUBLIC IS INCREASINGLY PRUDENT

Although the specifics of Iran's policies vary considerably, in almost all cases there has been a shift toward prudence.  Particularly near Iran's own borders, the Islamic regime has tended to support the status quo with regard to territorial integrity and has shown a preference for working with governments over substate movements.  Moreover, Iran has tried to contain unrest abroad and has tacitly supported repression by Turkey and Russia, even when this involved suppressing Muslims.  Tehran has also curtailed ties to most Islamist movements, keeping its network in tact but not pushing for the overthrow of governments.

Iran has also shown prudence in its military posture, including its quest for WMD.  Iran's military budgets have been modest, focused more on defense than on offense.  Despite the geostrategic and other imperatives driving Iran to acquire WMD, it has done so in a quiet and deliberate manner, avoiding alarm and preventing the United States from developing a strong coalition to stop its acquisition.

## IRAN INCREASINGLY USES IDEOLOGY AS A MASK FOR REALPOLITIK

Iran has long been willing to sacrifice its ideals for its national interest, but this tendency has increased in recent years.  Iran still supports Shi'a radicals and other Islamists throughout the world—and champions the anti-Israel front—but its motives and its priorities are increasingly dictated by cold national interest concerns.  Thus, it directs the Iraqi Shi'as against the MKO, tries to use the Palestinians to increase its leverage over the peace process, and otherwise uses proxies as means rather than ends.

## IRAN'S DECISIONMAKING IS CHAOTIC BUT NOT ANARCHIC

There are rules to Iran's decisionmaking on major security issues, but the rules appear to be in constant flux.  The rules are known to the players involved but never codified. The Iranian system and broader culture stress consensus and keep most major players involved in decisionmaking—a tendency reinforced by personal ties that cut across institutions. On most issues, many important players have a voice. In addition, the system emphasizes consensus, preventing individuals or small numbers of institutions from dominating the overall agenda or acting without higher approval. Even when individuals do not agree on the ultimate policy, a willingness to give and take and horse trade in general enables the policy process to move along, if fitfully.

## IMPLEMENTATION IS UNEVEN BUT SELDOM CONFLICTING

Because Iran's security institutions have overlapping responsibilities, they are often called upon to accomplish the same goals. Their different bureaucratic agendas and capabilities, however, often mean that they do so in quite different manners. At times, these efforts work in concert. With regard to Iraq, for example, the *Artesh* manages the conventional threat while the IRGC handles Iraqi resistance groups and Iranian dissidents. The emphasis on consensus, along with the relative lack of military autonomy, prevents too much deviation from agreed-upon objectives.

## IRAN'S SECURITY FORCES ARE SUBORDINATE TO CIVILIAN CONTROL

In general, Iran's security forces respect and follow the wishes of Iran's civilian leadership, even though they vigorously champion their own agendas whenever possible. Thus, on issues such as the Chemical Weapons Convention, the military will accept civilian decisions despite its preferences. Similarly, the overall military budget has been limited, despite the wishes of all the institutions. The IRGC in particular has been on the losing end of many bureaucratic battles in Iran in recent years. It has not, however, responded by trying "rogue operations," or otherwise acting without civilian approval.

There is no neat civilian and military split. Given the many disparate opinions often found within the security institutions, it is more common for parts of the security establishment to be allied with civilians against other factions.

## IRAN'S SECURITY FORCES PREFER SHOWS OF FORCE WHILE SEEKING TO AVOID ACTIVE CONFRONTATIONS

Iran's security forces, particularly the regular military, are often voices of restraint. In several of the most recent standoffs, most notably the confrontation with the Taliban after their murder of Iranian diplomats in Mazar-e Sharif, Iran's security forces have tried to avoid escalation even as they sought to project an image of strength. Thus, when tension threatened to escalate with Turkey and Iraq—and, most visibly, with the Taliban in 1998—Iran's military forces conducted maneuvers and buildups near the respective areas of conflict but deliberately sought to avoid open confrontation. The military forces fear that almost any broad conflict would be costly and deeply unpopular.

## DIFFERENCES BETWEEN IRAN'S REGULAR ARMED FORCES AND ITS REVOLUTIONARY ARMED FORCES ARE DECREASING

The once-clear distinction between the *Artesh* and the IRGC, while not gone, has diminished considerably in the last decade. Recruiting is now handled by a central authority. As the IRGC's commitment to professionalism has grown, and its Islamist ardor waned, it has increasingly conducted business in a manner similar to that of the *Artesh*.

## ISRAEL AND THE UNITED STATES REPRESENT EXCEPTIONS TO MANY GENERALIZATIONS

Iran's continued rejection of normalization with the United States and its strong ties to many rejectionist groups suggest that its general shift toward moderation does not apply universally. Restrictions on relations with both countries remain one of the strongest parts of the revolutionary legacy. Although raising the possibility of dialog with the United States is no longer taboo, Tehran still pursues an uncompromising policy toward Washington—far less pragmatic than its policy toward Iraq, which poses a greater immediate danger. Similarly, even though Iran's hostility toward Israel has lost its revolutionary edge, Tehran still exaggerates the threat Israel poses to its security.

## FINAL WORDS

This report has tried to provide insight into Iranian decisionmaking and overall security policy. One consistent finding is that the system is in flux. Our findings and analysis should serve as a base for further exploration, but not as the final word. Any conclusions should be recognized for what they are—tentative findings that will change as new players emerge in Iran and as political and strategic conditions change.

"A New China Embracing Nuclear Nonproliferation." *International Herald Tribune*, December 11, 1997, p. 1.

*Al-Ahram al-Yawm* (Amman), December 1, 1998. BBC ME/3398 MED/17.

Amini, Amir Houshang. "Iran's Standing in the Regional Geo-Economic Equation." *Iran Commerce* (Iran Chamber of Commerce, Industries and Mines), vol. 4, no. 2, Autumn 1997, pp. 20-24.

Amirahmadi, Hooshang, ed. *Revisiting Iran's Strategic Significance in the Emerging Regional Order.* New Brunswick, NJ: U.S.-Iran Conference, 1995.

Amuzegar, Jahangir. "Khatami and Iranian Economic Policy in the Mid-term." *The Middle East Journal*, vol. 53, no. 4, Autumn 1999, pp. 534-552.

Aqili, Parviz, Mussa Ghaninezad, Ali Jahankhani, and Heydar Pourian. "Getting Out of Economic Crisis Needs Courage: We Do Not Have Much Time." *Jameah*, May 9, 1998, p. 7.

Asghar, Ali, and Keivan Hosseni. "The US and the Technological Ban On Iran." *The Journal of Defence Policy* (*Siyasat-e Defa'i*), vol. 7, no. 1, Winter 1998/1999, pp. 49-68.

Bakhash, Shaul. *The Reign of the Ayatollahs: Iran and the Islamic Revolution.* London: I.B. Tauris, 1985.

Barzin, Saeed.   "Iran: Reining in the Right."   *Middle East International,* July 30, 1999, pp. 17-18.

Ben-Dor, Gabriel.  "Ethno-politics and the Middle Eastern State."  In Milton Esman and Itamar Rabinovich, eds., *Ethnicity, Pluralism and the State in the Middle East.*  Ithaca, NY: Cornell University Press, 1988.

Blitz, James. "D'Alema Seeks Positive Solution to Ocalan Dilemma." *Financial Times,* November 18, 1998.

Bokari, Farhan.  "Pakistan's Shias Live in Fear of Further Massacres." *Financial Times,* January 11, 1999.

Buchta, Wilfried.  *Who Rules Iran? The Structure of Power in the Islamic Republic.*  Washington, DC: Washington Institute for Near East Policy and Konrad Adenauer Stiftung, 2000.

Byman, Daniel L., and Roger Cliff.  *China's Arms Sales: Motivations and Implications.*  Santa Monica, CA: RAND, 1999.

*Canal-7* (Istanbul, in Turkish), June 16, 1997.   BBC ME/2949 MED/11-12, June 19, 1997.

Carus, Seth, and Michael Eisenstadt.   "Iran's Nuclear Weapons Program: Status and Implications." *Policywatch,* no. 444, March 8, 2000 (electronic version).

Chubin, Shahram.  *Iran's National Security Policy: Capabilities, Intentions and Impact.*  Washington, DC: Carnegie Endowment for International Peace, 1994.

Chubin, Shahram, and Charles Tripp.  *Iran and Iraq at War.*  London: I.B. Tauris, 1988.

Chubin, Shahram, and Charles Tripp.  "Iran-Saudi Relations and Regional Order." *Adelphi Paper,* no. 304.  London: IISS, 1996.

Constable, Pamela.  "Afghan Town Praises Iran as Nearby Border Opens to Trade." *International Herald Tribune,* December 23, 1999, p. 1.

Cordesman, Anthony. *Iran's Military Forces in Transition.*  Westport, CT: Praeger, 1999.

Cordesman, Anthony H., and Abraham R. Wagner. *The Lessons of Modern War—Volume II: The Iran-Iraq War.* Boulder, CO: Westview Press, 1990.

de Bellaigue, Christopher. "The Struggle for Iran." *New York Review of Books*, December 16, 1999, p. 54.

Ehteshami, Anoushiravan. *After Khomeini: The Iranian Second Republic.* London: Routledge, 1995.

Ehteshami, Anoushiravan. "Iran on the Eve of the New Millennium: Domestic and Regional Perspectives." *FAU Seminar 1997*, Copenhagen, Foreningen Af Udviklingsforskere I Danmark, 1997, pp. 31-47.

Eisenstadt, Michael. "Dilemmas for the U.S. and Iran." *Policywatch*, no. 414, October 8, 1999 (electronic version).

*Ettela'at International*, January 9, 1997.

Freij, Hanna Yousif. "State Interest vs. the Umma: Iranian Policy in Central Asia." *Middle East Journal*, vol. 50, no. 1, Winter 1996, pp. 71-83.

Fuller, Graham. *The "Center of the Universe."* Boulder, CO: Westview Press, 1991.

Gasiorowski, Mark. "The Power Struggle in Iran." *Middle East Policy*, Vol. VII, No. 4, October 2000.

Gill, Bates. *Silkworms and Summitry: Chinese Arms Exports to Iran.* New York: The Asia and Pacific Rim Institute of the American Jewish Committee, 1997.

Green, Jerrold D. "Iran: Limits to Rapprochement." Statement before the Senate Committee on Foreign Relations, Subcommittee on Near Eastern and South Asian Affairs, May 1999.

*Gulf States Newsletter*, vol. 24, no. 625, November 24, 1999.

Hiro, Dilip. *Iran Under the Ayatollahs.* London: Routledge and Keegan Paul, 1995.

Huyser, Gen. Robert E. *Mission to Tehran*. London: Andre Deutsch, 1986.

"India's Emerging Nuclear Threat to Persian Gulf Security." *Iranfile*, vol. 1, no. 5, February/March 1999, pp. 8-9.

International Institute for Strategic Studies (London, UK). *The Military Balance*, various years.

International Monetary Fund, *International Financial Statistics Yearbook*. Washington, DC: International Monetary Fund, 2000.

*Iran News*, February 6, 1998.

*Iran News*, April 28, 1997.

"Iran: Wrapping Up the Networks?" *Gulf States Newsletter*, vol. 25, no. 629, February 7, 2000, p. 2.

"Iran's Relations with the States of Central Asia and Transcaucasia." *Background Brief*. London: Foreign and Commonwealth Office, August 1998.

*IRNA*, February 23, 1999. BBC ME/3648 MED/8, February 25, 1999.

*IRNA* (Tehran), December 1, 1998. BBC ME/3400 MED/7-8, December 3, 1998.

*IRNA* (Tehran, in English), September 4, 1999. BBC ME/3632 MED/13, September 6, 1999.

Jaber, Hala. *Hezballah: Born with a Vengeance*. London: Fourth Estate, 1997.

Jaffee Center for Strategic Studies. *The Middle East Military Balance*, various years.

*Jameah*, April 29, 1998.

Jehl, Douglas. "Rage Rises in Iran Over Killing." *International Herald Tribune*, September 12, 1998, p. 9.

Kan, Shirley A. *Chinese Proliferation of Weapons of Mass Destruction: Current Policy Issues*. Washington, DC: Congressional Research Service Brief, March 23, 1998, p. 6.

*Kayhan*, December 10, 1996.

Kazemi, Farad. "Ethnicity and the Iranian Peasantry." In Milton Esman and Itamar Rabinovich, eds., *Ethnicity, Pluralism and the State in the Middle East*. Ithaca, NY: Cornell University Press, 1988.

Khalaf, Roula. "World Bank May Resume Iran Loans." *Financial Times*, January 29/30, 2000, p. 3.

Khatami, Mohammed. *IRNA*, December 1, 1998.

Lancaster, John. "U.S.: Iran's Terrorism Role Grows." *Washington Post*, December 4, 1999, p. 1 (electronic version).

*Le Monde*, July 20, 1999, p. 7.

Loftian, Saideh. "Iran's Middle East Policies Under President Khatami." *The Iranian Journal of International Affairs*, vol. X, no. 4, Winter 1998-1999, p. 34.

MacDonald, Charles. "The Kurdish Question in the 1980's." In Milton Esman and Itamar Rabinovich, eds., *Ethnicity, Pluralism and the State in the Middle East*. Ithaca, NY: Cornell University Press, 1988.

Menashri, David. "Whither Iranian Politics? The Khatami Factor." In Patrick Clawson et al., *Iran Under Khatami: A Political, Economic and Military Assessment*. Washington, DC: Washington Institute for Near East Policy, 1998, pp. 13-51.

Mesbahi, Mohiaddin. "Tajikistan, Iran and the International Politics of the 'Islamic Factor.'" *Central Asian Survey*, vol. 16, no. 2, 1997, pp. 141-158.

Nifisi, Azar. "Student Demonstrations in Iran: What's Next?" *Policywatch*, no. 400, July 21, 1999 (e-mail summary).

Norton, Augustus Richard. "Walking Between Raindrops: Hizballah in Lebanon." *Mediterranean Politics*, vol. 3, no. 1, Summer 1998.

Peterson, Scott. "Iran Opens Door—a Little—to U.S." *Christian Science Monitor*, February 25, 2000, p. 1.

Phillips, Alan. "Iranians Watch and Wait as Shi'ite Cousins Suffer." *Sunday Telegraph*, February 28, 1999, p. 21.

"Protests Near Tehran and in Southwest." Radio Free Europe/Radio Liberty, *Iran Report*, vol. 3, no. 2, January 10, 1999 (electronic version).

Quinlivan, James. "Coup Proofing: Its Practice and Consequences in the Middle East." *International Security*, vol. 24, no. 2, Fall 1999.

Radio Free Europe/Radio Liberty. *Iran Report*, vol. 2, no. 36, September 13, 1999.

Radio Free Europe/Radio Liberty. *Iran Report*, vol. 2, no. 45, December 15, 1999 (electronic version).

Radio Free Europe/Radio Liberty. *Iran Report*, vol. 3, no. 17, May 1, 2000.

Rafsanjani, Hashemi. *Vision of the Islamic Republic of Iran, Network 1* (Tehran). BBC ME/3304 MED/1-5, August 15, 1998.

Ranstorp, Magnus. "The Strategy and Tactics of Hizballah's Current 'Lebanonization Process.'" *Mediterranean Politics*, vol. 3, no. 1, Summer 1998, p. 118.

"Roundtable: New Geopolitical Developments in the Region and Iranian National Security." *Middle East Studies Quarterly* (Tehran), vol. 5, nos. 1-2, Summer and Fall 1998, pp. 5-54.

*Salam*, June 3, 1998.

Samii, A.W. "The Contemporary Iranian News Media, 1998-1999." *Middle East Review of International Affairs*, vol. 3, no. 4, December 1999 (electronic version).

Tarock, Adam. "Iran's Policy in Central Asia." *Central Asian Survey*, vol. 16, no. 2, 1997, pp. 185-200.

Valinejad, Afshin. "Iran Leader Calls for Israel's Annihilation." *Boston Globe*, January 1, 2000, p. 4.

Vatikiotis, P.G. "Non-Muslims in Muslim Societies." In Milton Esman and Itamar Rabinovich, eds., *Ethnicity, Pluralism and the*

*State in the Middle East.* Ithaca, NY: Cornell University Press, 1988.

*Vision of the Islamic Republic of Iran, Network 1* (Tehran, in Persian), October 31, 1999. BBC Summary of World Broadcasts, ME/3681 MED/7-8, November 2, 1999.

*Voice of the Islamic Republic of Iran,* August 9, 1998. BBC ME/3302 MED/21, August 11, 1998.

*Voice of the Islamic Republic of Iran* (Tehran), September 15, 1998. BBC ME/3334 MED, September 17, 1998.

*Voice of the Islamic Republic of Iran* (Tehran, in Persian), December 13, 1999. BBC ME/3720 MED/6-10, December 17, 1999, p. 9.

Zabih, Sepehr. *The Iranian Military in Revolution and War.* London: Routledge, 1988.

Dr. Daniel Byman is the Research Director of RAND's Center for Middle East Public Policy. He writes regularly on the Persian Gulf and other topics related to U.S. national security.

Dr. Shahram Chubin is Director of Research at the Geneva Centre for Security Policy, where he specializes in security issues, especially those relating to the Middle East.

Dr. Anoush Ehteshami is the Director of the Centre for Middle Eastern and Islamic Studies and Professor of International Relations at the University of Durham. He has authored and edited several books and has written numerous articles on Iran and on Middle East politics and security.

Dr. Jerrold D. Green is the Director of International Programs and Development and the Director of the Center for Middle East Public Policy at RAND. Dr. Green writes regularly on Iran and on Persian Gulf affairs.